Your Retirement Journey

Planning the NEXT chapter of your life

Cody Meeks

Time is free, but it is priceless.
You can't own it, but you can spend it.
Once you've lost it, you can never get it back.
                              ~ Harvey MacKay

CONTENTS

PROLOGUE

Inflection point: in·flec·tion point

Noun: a time of significant change in a situation; a turning point.

This is not a book about the COVID-19 pandemic. This is a book about what comes next. Specifically, this book addresses what you can do today to position your retirement for what the new future holds.

When the COVID-19 pandemic hit America in March of 2020, many of us thought about the weeks or months ahead. What changes would come? How soon would things go back to normal?

As the months went by, we came to realize some things are never going back to "normal."

Sure, the restrictions will end and the masks will eventually come off, but what will life look like? What about our sense of wellbeing? The way business is conducted? The trajectory of our economy? Our nation's public policy? The pandemic has irrevocably impacted all.

The COVID-19 pandemic was an inflection point that, by necessity, changes what comes after it.

It can feel new and scary – especially when it comes to your financial future. Let us start by acknowledging one thing: This is not the first inflection point for American savers, and it will not be the last.

We need to understand what makes this moment unique and how to make the necessary adjustments to growing, saving, and spending our wealth.

Americans have survived through historical challenges and changes to the economy and the stock market.

The Great Depression of the 1920s and '30s uncovered the fragility of an unregulated stock market. The OPEC embargo of the 1970s exposed America's reliance on foreign oil to power our economic engines. The technology bubble burst of the early 2000s showed the dangers of ballooning stock prices. The mortgage crisis of 2007-2008 gave pause to the American dream of growing wealth through homeownership.

None of these inflection points took down America's ability to save and prepare for the future. Still, they all required adjustments for savers who wanted to achieve their pre-crisis financial goals.

We are living in another inflection point as we move into the 2020s – one perhaps larger than anything our country has experienced since the Great Depression. The COVID-19 pandemic disrupted the American economy in ways not seen for generations. Jobs, commerce, and the markets have all been impacted in the U.S. and abroad.

But, as we will discuss in this book, there is reason for hope! In fact, like many inflection points, the COVID pandemic presents opportunities for those savers who understand the new risks being created and uncovered. Consider this book as a roadmap to navigating what comes next. Instructions on how you can reposition your retirement savings to overcome these new risks and achieve the happy retirement you deserve.

MEET THE AUTHOR

Cody Meeks was born in Dodge City, KS to Brad and Vickie Meeks. After relocating several times during his childhood due to his father's employment, he finally returned to Southwest Kansas at the age of 7 to a small town called Garden City. The move to Garden City was an inflection point in Cody's life. His grandparents, Ione and Melvin Louk resided in Garden City and quickly became a corner stone in Cody's life. He spent much of his childhood living with his grandparents. Learning the value of honesty, integrity but most importantly, the value of hard work. Ione and Melvin dedicated their lives to three things: faith, family and community and instilled those values into Cody from a young age. After working as an elementary secretary and elevator manager, Ione and Melvin retired in March of 2005 at the ages of 65 and 67.

After witnessing his grandmother and grandfather work tirelessly for their entire lives to provide for themselves and others, Cody was excited to watch his grandparents' transition into retirement! Unfortunately, 2008 hit the reset button on their financial future. Cody observed firsthand how quickly things can change. The conversations were no longer centered around, "where should we visit next," but rather about, "can we afford to stay retired?"

During the 2008 financial collapse, Cody was studying to become an Engineer at Washburn University in Topeka, KS, but could not stomach what was happening to his grandparents. He dropped everything and started his quest for financial knowledge. There had to be some way, something that could put his grandparents back on track.

After months of research, Cody realized his grandparents were not alone. Millions of Americans in or near retirement were now asking themselves the same questions. Can we still retire? What do we do? How do we recover?

It was in that moment that Cody had another inflection point. There are plenty of engineers in the world, but there are very few people helping individuals retire with confidence in their financial future. As you will learn from reading this book, there are two types of financial advisors. Wealth advisors and retirement planners. As you enter this next stage of your life, it is important that you understand the difference between the two.

Cody has dedicated his life to making sure no one faces the tough decisions his grandparents had to make and can truly live financially free in retirement.

Is this book for me?

Retirement is a long game, not a sprint. We need to prepare not just for the act of retiring, but for the length of retirement as well.

How do you play the long game when it comes to retirement?

The long game is all about identifying and executing steps today that set you up for long-term success tomorrow.

Put another way: When it comes to retirement, short-term wins matter far less than long-term gains.

If you are wondering if this book is for you, the answer is probably yes. The challenges that we will discuss in the coming chapters impact almost every American saver to some degree. There is a good chance you are underprepared for at least some of the challenges you are going to face in retirement.

CHAPTER 1:

Meet John and Diana

Beep, beep, beep, beep…

It's 4:00 a.m. and the only light illuminating the room is a faint blue glow coming from Diana's alarm clock.

She reaches over, trying to locate the snooze button for the alarm clock sitting on the nightstand beside her bed. Once she is finally able to silence the alarm, she gently removes the covers from her body and places her feet firmly on the floor. She slowly rolls out of bed and starts making her way to the master bathroom. Every step is deliberate. She does not want to wake her husband, John, if she can avoid it. John works the second shift for a construction company and has only been asleep for a few hours.

Diana and John are the typical "white picket fence" Americans. They got married early, at the age of 22 and 19, respectively. After finishing college, Diana applied to be an intern with Martin Marietta, which quickly transitioned into a full-time job. They soon started planning for a family and were blessed with two children, Ben and Lisa.

As their two children grew, Ben started to enjoy team sports and joined a soccer team. Lisa was a bit more reserved and enjoyed doing individual activities like reading and painting.

Soon, the kids were becoming adults and applying for different colleges. It was an exciting time for the entire family! Ben was accepted to the University of Denver where he began studying accounting. Lisa followed in her mother's footsteps and attended the School of Mines in Golden pursing a degree in engineering.

Even though John and Diana focused on building a bright future for their children, they also understood the importance of planning for themselves and their retirement. For the past 34 years, with every paycheck they received, 6 percent was automatically withdrawn and placed into their 401k Individual Retirement Account (IRA). Through good times and the bad, they stayed true to their plan. Both have always been goal-oriented people and their goals were simple.

- Pay off the house (which they had accomplished)
- Build their 401k to $1million (which they had just accomplished)
- Retire together on Diana's thirty-fifth anniversary with the company, which is now Lockheed-Martin

15

As Diana turned on the light in the master bathroom, she saw a calendar beside her mirror filled with red Xs crossing out the days. Only thirty-seven days remained until she and John accomplished their third and final goal, which was for both of them to retire on Diana's thirty-fifth anniversary with the company and unplug her alarm clock for good!

Standing in front of her mirror, she took the red Sharpie on the counter in front of the calendar and marked off the date, November 25, 1999. Diana placed the Sharpie back on the counter and looked at herself in the mirror. Under her breath she mumbled, "only 36 more days to go!"

As she stared into the mirror, the smile that had formed after marking off the date was slowly washed away. Reality was setting in. Diana only had 36 more days before she would walk out the doors of Lockheed-Martin and never go back.

"Are we actually ready?" Diana whispered to herself.

CHAPTER 2:

Are we ready?

If you go back in history a hundred years, the concept of retirement barely existed. If you were alive and able, you worked. When you quite working, it was likely because you were ill, injured, or dead.

All of that changed in the 1880s when Otto von Bismark, the minister president of Prussia, proposed government-funded financial support for the nation's oldest citizens. Germany eventually approved the plan, providing financial assistance to citizens who lived past age seventy. At the time, this financial assistance didn't amount to much because no one really lived that long!

Fast forward fifty years. America adopts the German idea of providing financial assistance to its aging population by creating the Social Security system. When the concept was initially adopted, the retirement age for Americans was sixty-five. During this time period, in 1935, the average life expectancy of an American was only fifty-eight.

By the 1970s, life expectancies in the U.S. increased to seventy. Every year since then, life expectancies in the United States has continued to increase. As of today, a 65-year-old should expect to live 25+ years, nearly 1/3rd of their lives in retirement.

While you are working, retirement planning seemed simple. Automatically deduct a certain percentage from your paycheck and have it directly deposited into your 401k. Even though the stock market has its bad years, the good years far outweigh the bad! Just "ride out" the dips and focus on the long-term goal of growing your 401k as much as possible!

As financial planners, we call this the accumulation phase. The only goal you have is to accumulate as much wealth as possible so that you can live off that wealth in retirement. Because you only have one goal, the strategy to accomplish that goal is simple. Build the best strategy that accomplishes growth!

Now let's shift your focus to your retirement years. Do you still only have one goal?

Of course, not! When you walk out of your employer's door for the last time, that is also the last time you will automatically receive that paycheck directly deposited into your checking account. Overnight, your goals have changed. You are no longer focusing on accumulating wealth—you are now distributing your wealth. Instead of adding to your retirement accounts regularly, you will now be depleting those accounts regularly.

Because your goals have changed, your strategies must change as well!

When I am meeting with clients, I walk them through what I call my "Retirement Journey Checklist." The first step is to make sure you outline all of your goals.

- How much income do you need monthly to sustain your lifestyle?
- What sources of income do you currently have?
  - Social Security
  - Rentals
  - Pension (some of you are still lucky enough to have a pension)
  - Investments
- What bucket list items do you want to accomplish while you are still able?
- What are you currently doing to accomplish these goals?

You may notice, I did not ask you how long you are going to live. If you knew the answer to that question, retirement planning would be simple! (but no one does…)

After getting an outline of what is important to you and what goals you have for retirement, I draw four vertical lines on the white board and name the sections Goals, Strategies, Tools with space underneath to write.

Goals	Strategies	Tools

Many of the couples I meet with have similar goals.

- We need $5,000 per month to feel comfortable
- We would like to spend $8,000-$10,000 per year traveling
- If there is anything left over, we would like to leave it to our kids/grandkids

Sound familiar?

Let's fill in the "Retirement Journey Checklist" with the goals

Goals	Strategies	Tools
- Income: $5,000/month - Travel: $8,000-$10,000 per year - Legacy		

Now think about your current situation because your goals will be similar. What strategies are you currently implementing to achieve those goals?

If you are unsure of your strategy, refer to your conversations with your current advisor. What do you spend most of your time talking about when you sit down to review your retirement plan?

If I had to guess, I'd say most of your time is spent on the tools section.

- "Well Mr. and Mrs. Client, we have you diversified between 40 percent bonds and 60 percent stocks. We have both international and domestic exposure using these various exchange-traded fund (ETF) accounts and we are reducing your risk by protecting 40 percent in high-yielding bond funds."

Does that sound familiar?

From my experience, most financial advisors only focus on the tools section. They ask you seven to ten questions trying to determine your tolerance for "risk" then build a "custom portfolio" specifically designed for your tolerance for "risk."

Once the portfolio is built, they typically spend some time discussing how your portfolio would have reacted throughout history and once all of that is done, they provide you a probability report showing you the chances of having a successful retirement.

Let us review the "Retirement Journey Checklist." After spending an hour with the typical financial advisor, what have you accomplished?

- You established your goals for retirement (at least I hope)
- You spent some time discussing various tools (most of which you probably did not understand)
- And then came up with a strategy to build a model portfolio based on your risk tolerance

Goals	Strategies	Tools
- Income: $5,000/month - Travel: $8,000-$10,000 per year - Legacy	- ???	- Domestic ETFs - International ETFs - Bond Funds - Commodities - Annuities: Fixed, Variable, Indexed - Checking/Savings - CDs - Real Estate

What strategies did you discuss? What are you going to implement together to improve your odds of having a successful retirement? How do those strategies move you closer to your goals?

This is not a trick question—I want you to be honest with yourself and ask, what are our current strategies for retirement?

If you really think about it, the meetings you are currently having only focus on which tools you are using to build a "risk-based" growth strategy. Is that a bad thing? Well, it depends on whether growing your portfolio is your only goal.

If your goals include having a travel fund or a specific amount of income each month or possibly leaving money behind for the next generation, those goals all require their own strategies to help you accomplish them!

Let me quickly break down each goal—I will cover each strategy in more detail in separate chapters.

So, you have a defined income goal of $5,000/month. How are you going to get there? What strategies do you need?

First thing we must do is determine each source of income you will have:

- Social Security: When should you file and why?
- Pension: Single life or joint life payments?
- Any other sources of income such as rent, annuities, royalties, etc.?

If your goal is to have a monthly income stream to pay the bills, you need an income strategy!

So, what goes into an income strategy? More than you think. Not only do we have to determine how much you need to be withdrawing from your portfolio, but we also have to plan for all of the "what-ifs" that could alter that plan.

Possible "what-ifs" that you need to have a strategy for:

- What if one spouse predeceases the other? How will that affect your Social Security payments? How will your pension payments be affected? Will you have to pay more in taxes as a single individual?

Having a complete income strategy means you have planned for much more than just how much you need each month. You have built a strategy around taxes, survivor's benefits, inflation. If done correctly, your income strategy should protect you from anything life can possibly throw your way over the next twenty-five or more years.

Goals	Strategies	Tools
- Income: $5,000/month - Travel: $8,000-$10,000 per year - Legacy	- Risk-Based Growth Strategy - Income Strategy - Tax Strategy - Inflation Strategy - Survivor Strategy - Downside Protection Strategy - Healthcare Strategy - Estate Planning Strategy	- Domestic ETFs - International ETFs - Bond Funds - Commodities - Annuities: Fixed, Variable, Indexed - Checking/Savings - CDs - Real Estate

Although your goals may seem simple, the strategies needed to help you accomplish those goals are extremely complex.

The only way to enjoy a comfortable retirement—a retirement in which you can truly disconnect and not worry about money—is to have a comprehensive plan that uses a variety of strategies focused on your goals.

Although you are currently diversified among several different tools inside of your retirement accounts, this alone will not ensure you have a successful retirement.

CHAPTER 3

Starting Their Journey

Remember John and Diana?

January 3, 2000 was the first business day of the new year. Although both John and Diana entered retirement together, Diana's alarm still went off at 4:00 am. She began her normal routine reaching over for the alarm clock—stumbling to find the snooze button—rolling out of bed and entering the master bathroom to start getting ready for work.

Her body had done this routine for so long, Diana did not even realize it was unnecessary until she turned on the bathroom light and noticed a rose sitting on the counter next to a letter from John.

Congrats, Diana! It is hard to believe how fast the past thirty five years have gone. Although I have enjoyed every minute of it with you, I'm most excited to spend the next thirty years waking up next to you. Come back to bed and let's start the rest of our lives together.

~ Love, John

Diana wiped the tears from her face and quietly walked back into the bedroom and went back to bed, excited to start the next chapter of their life—together!

Due to Diana being the larger earner, most of their retirement savings were in her 401k account. Although she had the largest account, she HATED finances and let John handle everything. This honestly worked out to their benefit! Just ten years from retirement, heading into 1990, the two of them had only saved $487,000. With the goal of $1 million saved before retirement, they were unsure if they would make it.

John started educating himself on the stock market and took full control over both of their retirement accounts. Although their investment options were limited inside of their 401k accounts, he followed the different trends in the early-1990s and jumped in and out of different funds that were doing well. By 1996, the accounts had grown to nearly $700,000! John's efforts were paying off big-time! By 1999, they had exceeded their $1 million goal—they had reached $1.1 million!

Because of how incredibly successful John had been growing their accounts, Diana never questioned letting him continue to manage her funds. Especially now that he could manage their wealth from the kitchen table instead of the cab of a dump truck!

Since neither of them wanted to claim Social Security yet, the $5,000 a month or $60,000 a year they needed to sustain their lifestyle would have to be taken exclusively from their retirement savings. Most economist will warn retirees that you should never withdraw more than 4 percent from your portfolio per year in retirement. Once you factor in taxes, John and Diana were going to take nearly 6 percent!

You must remember, 2000 was a different time. The stock market had averaged 14 percent per year for the past decade. Banks were offering 7 percent interest on CDs. Plus, it was only short-term! John was 61 and would be eligible for Social Security soon.

As the year progressed, the stock market started to experience some volatility, but that did not concern John. The stock market "always" goes up over time! This soon will pass. By the end of 2000, John and Diana had $940,000 of their original $1,100,000 left.

Diana, completely unaware of their financial situation, suggested that she and John might start some home improvement projects. They had been in their current house more than 30 years and never really had the money to make it "their own." She had always dreamed about remodeling the kitchen and master bathroom.

Since this was their forever home, John agreed it was time to make it everything they had ever wanted. After collecting several bids,

Diana found the perfect contractor who said he could get her everything she wanted for $50,000.

The contractor got to work—but quickly exceeded the budget (as contractors sometimes do). The final project ended up costing $70,000. John and Diana had some money in their savings account, but it was not anywhere near enough to pay for the remodel. After having some lengthy discussions, John informed Diana it was best to take it from her 401k. The two of them had started retirement $100,000 ahead of their goal. Taking $70,000 would not be a big deal in the grand scheme of things.

What John hadn't calculated was the amount of taxes that would be owed on withdrawing that amount. You see, when you have tax-deferred assets like a 401k or IRA, you have never paid Uncle Sam his portion. You don't pay the taxes until you take funds from the account as a distribution.

They had now withdrawn $130,000 ($70,000 for the remodel plus $60,000 living expenses). After calculating how much taxes were owed, both state and federal, John realized that he would need to take an additional $22,000 for taxes. Meaning that in 2001, just the second year into their retirement, they withdrew $152,000.

Let us not forget, 2001 was not a favorable year for the stock market. Like the year 2000, 2001 ended down just shy of 12 percent.

What was $1.1 million two years ago, was now worth $695,025. But that was ok! Although John was starting to get somewhat concerned with how much money they had spent/lost in the first two years of retirement—it was not anything to panic about.

To try and get things back on track, John started devoting more time to their portfolios. He started reading more about different companies and listening to the news/investment experts to determine the best strategy to take. After two years of declines, John determined that 2002 would be an up year in the stock market and moved their investments to nearly 100 percent in equities to capture the potential growth.

Early on, it appeared to be working! Their retirement accounts were finally going in the right direction and growing again!

Diana asked John if they could plan their first big trip together now that the house was completed. July seemed like the best time to go. So, they started planning. They wanted to start in London, then go to Paris, and finish their trip in Rome. The total cost would be around $15,000. They booked the trip and began sharing the news!

John, dedicated now more than ever to their retirement accounts spent day and night on his computer reading opinions of what was going on. Everything was recovering well after what happened on Sept. 11th. But now all the sudden things were shifting. For some reason, the market was starting to go down again.

Although he was stressed, John did not let Diana know about their situation. They continued to plan for their trip. As best he could, John tried to act like everything was business as usual.

In the week leading up to their departure, the stock market began to crash. In just five trading days the Dow Jones had dropped nearly 600 points (which was a lot back then!) While in Paris, John noticed a newspaper headline that read "The Stock Market Continues to Crash" on their way to dinner. Although John tried to act like everything was normal, Diana noticed that something was off with him.

While sitting at a romantic restaurant on what was supposed to be their first real vacation together since Ben and Lisa were born, John told Diana the truth. At that very moment, they only had $416,000 left of what was $1.1 million just two years prior.

CHAPTER 4

Sequence of Returns

What went wrong for John and Diana?

Although it is impossible to predict when and to what degree the stock market will turn negative during your years in retirement, it is vital to your success that you have a plan to protect yourself from it. Most retirees will face two if not three recessions during their years in retirement.

During the '90s, John did an amazing job putting together a growth strategy for their retirement accounts. Unfortunately, John had zero experience managing downside risk. When the stock market started to crash, instead of implementing a downside protection plan he relied on his previous knowledge of the market which is to just "hold on" and "ride it out."

Although this philosophy holds true and the stock market does recover over time, the two things that John had not factored into their plan were:

1) Sequence of Returns Risk

2) Rate of Return Variance

In this chapter, I will explain both and why they are critical to your success.

What do I mean when I say, Sequence of Returns Risk?

- As defined by Investopedia

> Sequence risk is the danger that the timing of withdrawals from a retirement account will have a negative impact on the overall rate of return available to the investor. This can have a significant impact on a retiree who is taking withdraws from an account and is no longer contributing new capital that could offset losses. Sequence risk is also called sequence-of-returns risk.

OK—What does that mean in English?

Essentially, if you are taking distributions from an account, the order in which you receive gains and experience losses has a major impact. This is a completely new concept when you enter retirement. While you are working, if you are not taking withdraws from your retirement funds, it does not matter when you experience years of growth verse years of losses

Example:

Let us assume you have $500,000 invested starting in the year 2000

Year	S&P 500 Return	Portfolio Balance
2000	-9.27%	$453,662
2001	-12.11%	$398,728
2002	-21.51%	$308,986
2003	+29.21%	$399,235
2004	+11.08%	$443,472
2005	+5.1%	$466,089
2006	+16.08%	$541,040
2007	+5.59%	$571,291
2008	-37.68%	$356,019
2009	+26.95%	$451,957
2010	+15.34%	$521,276

After ten years in the stock market, you would have earned an average rate of return of 2.53 percent. Your accounts would have started with $500,000 and you would have ended with $521,276 if you took ZERO withdraws during that ten-year period from your accounts.

Let us take the same example but reverse the order in which you received the returns. Starting in 2010, then 2009, and ending in the year 2000.

Year	S&P 500 Return	Portfolio Balance
2010	+15.34%	$576,687
2009	+26.95%	$732,089
2008	-37.68%	$456,227
2007	+5.59%	$481,735
2006	+16.08%	$559,202
2005	+5.10%	$587,721
2004	+11.08%	$652,843
2003	+29.21%	$843,528
2002	-22.51%	$653,674
2001	-12.11%	$574,520
2000	-9.27%	$521,276

Even with the stock market returns reversed, you would have earned the same 2.53% average rate of return and you would have ended with the exact same amount.

Therefore, if you "hold on" and don't "panic sell" you will recover from your losses over time.

The key difference between your working years and being retired is that most people NEED to take distributions from their accounts and do not understand the consequences of sequence of returns because they have never had to deal with it before.

Let's do the same exercise, but this time assume you need $30,000 a year to supplement your income per year adjusted at 2 percent inflation.

Year	S&P Return	Withdrawal	Portfolio Balance
2000	-9.27%	-$30,000	$423,662
2001	-12.11%	-$30,600	$341,761
2002	-21.51%	-$31,212	$233,628
2003	+29.21%	-$31,836	$270,031
2004	+11.08%	-$32,473	$267,478
2005	+5.1%	-$33,122	$247,997
2006	+16.08%	-$33,785	$254,093
2007	+5.59%	-$34,461	$233,839
2008	-37.68%	-$35,150	$110,575
2009	+26.95%	-$35,835	$104,519
2010	+15.34%	-$36,570	$83,980

If you complete these exercises starting in the year 2000, you would be left with $83,980 of your original $500,000 account after just ten years!

Earlier, when you were not taking withdrawals from the account, you averaged 2.53 percent regardless of when you experienced positive years in the market versus negative years. What happens if we reverse the returns? Let's say we start this exercise again but use the returns from 2010, then 2009, and so on. You will still have the same average rate of return of 2.53% over the ten-year period just like before, but will you end with the same dollar amount like you did before?

Year	S&P Return	Withdrawal	Portfolio Balance
2010	+15.34%	-$30,000	$546,687
2009	+26.95%	-$30,600	$663,405
2008	-37.68%	-$31,212	$382,212
2007	+5.59%	-$31,836	$371,745
2006	+16.08%	-$32,473	$399,052
2005	+5.10%	-$33,122	$386,282
2004	+11.08%	-$33,785	$395,298
2003	+29.21%	-$34,461	$476,298
2002	-22.51%	-$35,150	$333,947
2001	-12.11%	-$35,853	$257,657
2000	-9.27%	-$36,570	$197,208

Nope! If you use the returns from 2000 moving forward, you end up with $83,980. Using the same stock market returns but in reverse, starting with the year 2010, you end up with $197,208! That is more than a $100,000 difference in just a ten-year period! How can that be?

Simply put, when you do not take distributions from an account, the order in which the market has good years versus bad years does not matter—you never have to "sell" in order to pay the mortgage or utilities.

When you retire, and need to withdraw from these accounts, you can no longer "hold on" while the market is experiencing a loss. You still must sell in order to pay the bills! From my experience, the bank does not really care if you just suffered a 40 percent loss in your retirement accounts. They still want their payment!

So how do we plan for sequence of return risk in retirement?

We start by reducing your overall risk. In technical terms, this is defined as your variance. This is also known as the difference between a good year in the market and a bad year in the market.

Let us use another example to explain variance as it relates to investing.

- Example: Account value of $1,000,000
  - Year 1: The account grows by 25 percent
    - Account value after year 1 = $1,250,000
  - Year 2: The account grows by 20 percent
    - Account value after year 2 = $1,500,000

After just two years, your account has grown by 50 percent!

Congratulations!

Now let's assume that in year 3, you suffer your negative year in the stock market, and you lose some of its value. If your account grew by 50 percent in two years, it is safe to assume you are taking significant risk within those accounts. For this example, let's assume you lose 35 percent in year 3.

Before we calculate your account value after 3 years, let's first calculate your "average rate of return" since that is what most traditional wealth advisors focus on when they meet with clients.

- Year 1 = 25 percent growth
- Year 2 = 20 percent growth
- Year 3 = 35 percent loss
    o 25% + 20% - 35% = 10% Growth

Now, divide the 10 percent growth by the three years that the funds have been invested.

- 10% / 3 years = 3.33%

Over the three-year period, you earned 3.33 percent as an average rate of return. Not great, but hey you made money, right?

Instead of focusing on average rate of returns, let's instead calculate what your account would be worth.

Example: Account value of $1,000,000

- Year 1: The account grows by 25 percent
  - Account value after year 1 = $1,250,000
- Year 2: The account grows by 20 percent
  - Account value after year 2 = $1,500,000
- Year 3: The account suffers a 35 percent loss
  - Account value after year 3 = $975,000

Wait a second! Hold on.

You "averaged" a positive 3.33% rate of return over the three-year period BUT you lost money? How is that possible?

A couple of things

1) Average rate of return does not matter. Stop letting your advisor get away with talking about average rate of returns!
2) This exercise proves the old saying, "losses hurt more than gains."

Look at the chart below:

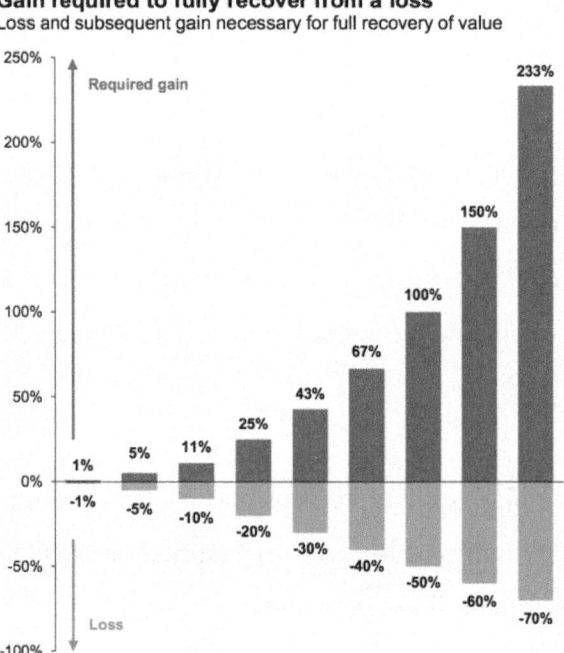

Gain required to fully recover from a loss
Loss and subsequent gain necessary for full recovery of value

This chart demonstrates the percentage of gains you would need to offset a loss. This means if you suffer a 20 percent loss, it requires a 25 percent gain to get you back to your original amount. A 30 percent loss requires a 43 percent gain to bring you back to even.

This is why you could experience 45 percent growth in the previous example (25 percent year 1 and 20 percent year 2) and only suffer a 35 percent loss and STILL lose money!

In retirement planning, this is an extremely important principle to understand. You can be fortunate to experience a long bull run in the market like what we have experienced since 2008 and give up a large portion of those gains because you have not changed your investment strategy.

This is what happened to John and Diana. John was extremely successful growing their accounts but never changed his investment strategy once he achieved their $1 million goal. He instead continued to implement a growth strategy that ultimately put their retirement at risk.

How can you alter your retirement plan to avoid falling victim to this mistake? Simple—Shift your investment strategy to focus on variance rather than on average rate of returns!

What is "variance"?

> The term **variance** refers to a statistical measurement of the spread between numbers in a data set. More specifically, **variance** measures how far each number in the set is from the mean and thus from every other number in the set.

Again, we need a translation into plain English!

Simply put, variance is the difference between your average rate of return (mean) and the best/worst years that got you to your average.

In our previous example, there is a BIG difference between earning 25 percent in one year and losing 35 percent the next. Positive 25 percent and negative 35 percent are a long way from your average rate of return, which was 3.33 percent.

What if we do the same exercise, but instead focus on reducing your variance? In other words, we focus on reducing the dramatic swings from positive years versus negative years.

Let's use $1,000,000 again for this example.

- Year 1: The account grows by 8 percent
  - Account value after year 1 = $1,080,000
- Year 2: The account grows by 4 percent
  - Account value after year 2 = $1,123,200
- Year 3: The account loses 2 percent
  - Account value after year 3 = $1,100,736

If we first calculate your average rate of return (8% + 4% - 2% = 10%) then divide by three years (10% / 3 = 3.33%) you will notice that you had the exact same average return during the three-year period as before of 3.33 percent.

Both examples had the same average. Both examples experienced two good years followed by a third year that experienced a loss.

Somehow, the second example has an account value of $125,000 more than the first example. How is that possible?

Sometimes, having a low-risk portfolio is a good thing! Not just for your peace of mind, but also for your wallet!

Now that we have explored two different principles of math, "sequence of returns" and "variance," think about your conversations with your current advisor. Have either of these topics ever come up?

If not, you are probably working with what we call a "wealth advisor."

What is a wealth advisor, you might ask?

A wealth advisor typically only focuses on the first phase of your life, the accumulation phase. That is the phase in which these two principles of math do not matter near as much.

Is that a bad thing?

Not necessarily. If you are still in the accumulation phase and your only goal is to grow your wealth, that is okay! But if you are reading this book, I am guessing that you are either retired now or planning to retire soon.

If you are transitioning to a different phase of your life, a phase that requires different strategies because your goals have changed, it might make sense to evaluate whether or not your financial advisor should be changed as well.

CHAPTER 5

Independent versus Captive

If you Google, "Financial Advisors—Denver, CO" you will get 16,400,000 search results (as of May of 2021) and more individuals are entering the profession every day.

So where do you begin your search for a new financial advisor?

Obviously, you are not going to call everyone from your google search—so where do you begin?

First, there are a few general categories into which we can separate financial advisors.

The first category is defined as a "captive" financial advisor. What does "captive" mean? Simply put, a captive financial advisor works for someone else. Think Edward Jones, Raymond James, and TransAmerica.

A captive advisor works for a company, which in some ways is great! Captive companies have large scale so they have multiple branches you can visit—they have typically been in business for a long period of time. They have a 1-800 number you can call 24/7. Don't get me wrong, there are some advantages to working with a captive advisor!

But we also must think about the disadvantages as well. If an advisor works for a parent company like Edward Jones or TransAmerica, is the advisor putting your best interest first or the company's interest? Well, that should be obvious, right? Of course, your needs are the most important thing to your advisor, and your advisor is going to build your portfolio based on those needs!

Yes, if an advisor is captive, he or she is going to do the best job possible building a plan around those needs. Unfortunately, because the advisor is captive, there are some restrictions in what tools the advisor can use to build your plan.

Think about it this way. If you are working with a TransAmerica advisor and are needing an annuity or life insurance product, do you think you will be offered products from other companies that are not TransAmerica? Of course not! All your "options" are going to be based on the company where that advisor works. That does not necessarily mean it will not accomplish your goals, but from my experience it might not be the "best" option or tool. There are hundreds of life insurance companies and annuity options available—if your advisor is captive, he or she is essentially handcuffed to the company where they work and are not even allowed to explore those other options with you.

What if you are not interested in life insurance or annuities? You only care about the stock market.

Well, first, I think of investments like a tool. A hammer is good at driving a nail but is not so good at loosening a pipe under the sink. You might be able to get that pipe loose using a hammer, but there are probably better tools that you could use to accomplish your goal. Don't enter retirement with a closed mind about certain investment tools. Every investment decision has both pros and cons. My goal is to educate you on your options and how those tools accomplish goals differently.

Okay, I am off my soap box!

What if you still do not care about alternative investments and you simply want to invest in the stock market? The stock market is the same stock market for everyone, right?

Yes, that is correct. Everyone has the same opportunity to invest in the same companies regardless of who they work with. Some advisors might have special investment opportunities like IPOs (initial public offerings) or private equity opportunities; but for the most part, all advisors offer the same opportunities for the stock market in general. When you buy Apple shares from advisor A, they are the same Apple shares you would buy from advisor B.

So, if all you care about is the stock market, does captive versus independent matter?

Simply put, yes—and here is why.

Most financial advisors do not purchase individual stocks. It takes a lot of time and research to invest in individual companies. A company doing well today can easily change direction and be doing worse tomorrow. To offset the time needed to research individual companies and build a portfolio for each client, most advisors use mutual funds.

What is a mutual fund?

> A mutual fund is a type of financial vehicle made up of a pool of money collected from many investors to invest in securities like stocks, bonds, money market instruments, and other assets.
> Source: www.investopedia.com/terms/m/mutualfund.asp (accessed 4.9.2021)

In other words, a financial planner hires an outside firm (a mutual fund company) to do the research and investing for them! That away, the financial planner simply invests a portion of your funds with the mutual fund company and bingo! Your account is now on autopilot!

This is where the difference starts to become apparent. Just like with insurance companies, there are thousands and thousands of mutual fund companies that provide this service for investors.

Let's do an experiment. If you are working with a financial advisor, take a quick look at your monthly statement. The first couple of pages are just the summary pages that show your account numbers and values. Keep going. You will eventually come to the pages of your statement that break down how your assets are invested. You might only see five different investments; you might see 200. This is what your advisor refers to as "diversification." Not all your assets are invested in the same thing.

What do you notice though, especially when you get to the mutual fund section?

Are all your mutual funds offered by the same company?
If they are, this is another clue that you are working with a captive advisor. You see, the advisor can offer only the mutual fund companies that the parent company allows. Again, your advisor will do the best he or she can to select the different funds that best meet your goals and objectives, but is handcuffed to the offerings of the

parent company.

This leads me to my final comparison of a captive financial planner versus an independent financial planner—conflict of interest. If the advisor you are working with is captive, with limited ability to invest your funds based on what the parent company allows, isn't that a conflict of interest? Isn't the advisor being forced to place the parent company ahead of your own best interest?

I hate to say it, but yes—and these companies know that it is a conflict of interest!

You see, unfortunately in life you can typically tell why someone recommends one thing versus another simply by understanding how that person gets paid. Put another way, if you walk into a Toyota dealership and tell the salesperson that you are deciding between buying a Toyota or a Ford, how many positive things do you think that salesperson is going to say about Ford?

My guess is ZERO. I could be wrong, but I am guessing that you are going to be told how Toyota holds its value better. That Toyotas are good for 300,000 miles versus Ford at 150,000 miles. You are going to hear every reason in the book as to why Toyotas are far superior to Fords.

If you hop in your car and drive to the Ford dealership and tell the salesperson that you just came from the Toyota dealership and are deciding between the two, now what are you going to hear?

The story is going to reverse—not because either vehicle is necessarily better than the other, but because the salesperson from Ford cannot sell a Toyota. If you decide you would rather go with the Toyota, the Ford salesperson is not going to make any money! The salespeople must convince you that their product is better for you than the competition, so they can get paid.

That is 100 percent a conflict of interest and that is the situation in which captive advisory firms place their advisors. The person you are working with could be the nicest person on the planet doing the absolute best job for you, but at the end of the day, he or she is handcuffed because of the employer.

Besides simply limiting your investment opportunities to a handful of mutual fund companies, it gets slightly worse when you evaluate how those mutual fund companies "compensate" the captive agencies.

What do I mean by that?

As I said, there are thousands and thousands of mutual fund companies throughout the world. Why would an advisor select one mutual fund company over another for all their clients?

Sometimes it is as easy as following the money…

Financial advisors get paid a variety of ways. Some charge a flat fee. Others charge you a percentage of the assets being managed. Although reducing your fees is important, you must pay for financial advice. No one can work for free.

One of the problems with the financial services industry is that not all fees are disclosed to the client. The advisor might state you are paying XYZ, but is that really everything that you are paying?

Let's circle back to mutual funds again quickly. Remember, mutual funds are investments that are purchased from a company. That company is employing individuals to research and build a portfolio. When you purchase shares from that mutual fund company, you are investing money into the portfolio that they built. Guess what? Mutual fund companies must make money as well to pay their employees and generate profits. Where do you think that money comes from?

You—plain and simple!

You pay a fee to invest in their mutual funds. These mutual fund costs are charged to you in a variety of different ways:

1) A-Shares: Mutual funds that carry a front-end load or sales charge

2) B-Shares: Mutual funds that carry a back-end load or sales charge

3) Expense Ratios: Internal costs charged to the investor

How do you know if you own A-Share or B-Share mutual funds inside of your portfolio? Typically, your statement will tell you! Since you already have it out, look at your individual investments. You will see a long name that identifies the company in which the mutual fund is purchased—American Funds, Blackrock, Franklin Templeton, and so on. You will then see the goal of the fund: balanced, income, growth. Then you might see one more item at the end of each mutual fund you own.

- Example:
  o American Funds American Balanced Fund® Class A

       ↑   ↑

    Company   Strategy

Guess what "Class A" stands for?

If you guessed, A-Shares, you are correct! You pay what is called a front-loaded sales charge to buy those mutual funds. If you have "Class B," you have not been charged yet, but you will pay the sales charge when you sell those mutual funds.

Which is better: paying your sales charge up front (A-Shares) or paying when you sell (B-Shares)?

I would argue neither!

The average sales charge/commission for investing funds into an A-Share or B-Share is between 3 percent and 5.5 percent. That is pretty dang expensive!

If you do not have "Class A" or "Class B" listed behind your mutual funds on your statement, that does not mean those investments are free. They just charge their fees a little differently. This is an area of financial planning where I take issue. At least Class A and Class B mutual funds disclose the sales charge that you will pay prior to investing. When a mutual fund company charges their fees via the "expense ratio" method, it is a bit more challenging.

Expense ratios differ from loaded mutual funds because the expense ratio is charged continuously while you are invested in the fund, not just on the front end or back end. Every mutual fund (even A-Shares and B-Shares) will carry some form of internal expense ratio, but not all are created equal.

You have probably seen the commercials on TV that advertise 0.04

percent expense ratio ETFs from Vanguard and a handful of other companies. ETFs differ slightly from mutual funds as they are passively managed and are designed simply to track an index. Because there is not much time and research put into managing the fund, they can be offered at a significant discount to mutual funds.

Nothing in life is free—you must pay for goods and services that are provided to you. Actively managed mutual funds can benefit clients during extreme periods of volatility to try and reduce downside risk and capture more upside, but what does that cost you?

Actively managed mutual funds can cost you anywhere between 0.15 percent to as high as 2.5 percent. Again, this is an internal fee that you pay for the duration of owning the mutual fund. This fee comes out prior to the company posting your gains and losses, meaning you never see it. What we do not see, we typically do not think about!

The difference between 0.15 percent and 2.5 percent is HUGE! Why would an advisor ever recommend a mutual fund that is so expensive? Over 15 or 20 years that adds up to a big difference! Well, you must follow the money … again.

Some mutual fund companies participate in what is known in the financial industry as "revenue sharing." What is revenue sharing you might ask?

Revenue sharing is the practice of adding additional non-investment related fees to the expense ratio of a mutual fund. These additional fees are then paid out to various service providers.

Source: https://www.employeefiduciary.com/blog/revenue-sharing-is-on-the-decline-in-401k-plans

(accessed 4/28/2021).

That is, revenue sharing is an *ADDITIONAL* fee added into the mutual fund expense ratio that has nothing to do with the fund itself. In nonfinancial terms, you are charged an additional fee (that you do not see, nor does it benefit you) so that a fee can be passed down to the advisor/firm that recommended that mutual fund to you.

How is this legal? How can you be charged fees without them being disclosed?

Well, it is disclosed to you. It is inside of those more than 300-page disclosure statements and prospectuses that you received. If those are provided to you when you are making your investment decisions, that is the only legal obligation that is required of your financial advisor. In the financial world, you are expected not only to read those disclosure statements, but you are also expected to understand them.

How bad could it be, you might be asking?

Here is an excerpt from the revenue sharing disclosure statement for Edward Jones:

Revenue Sharing Disclosure:

Edward D. Jones & Co., L.P. ("Edward Jones") is a registered broker-dealer and investment advisor in the United States and is wholly owned by the Jones Financial Companies, L.L.L.P. ("JFC"). Edward Jones receives payments known as revenue sharing from certain mutual fund companies, 529 plan program managers and insurance companies (collectively referred to as "product partners"). Virtually all of Edward Jones' transactions relating to mutual funds, 529 plans and annuity products involve product partners who pay revenue sharing to Edward Jones. We do not receive revenue sharing payments on assets within investment advisory programs. We want you to understand that Edward Jones' receipt of revenue sharing payments creates a potential conflict of interest in the form of an additional financial incentive and financial benefit to the firm, our financial advisors and equity owners in connection with the sale of products from these product partners. For the year that ended on December 31st, 2020, Edward Jones received revenue sharing payments of approximately $247.9 million from mutual fund and 529 product partners and $4.7 million from annuity product partners.

Source:
https://www.edwardjones.com/sites/default/files/acquiadam
/2021-02/revenue-sharing-disclosure.pdf
(accessed 5/29/2021).

Let's break down a few of the sentences that I have highlighted from the revenue disclosure provided by Edward Jones.

Virtually all of Edward Jones' transactions relating to mutual funds, 529 plans and annuity products involve product partners who pay revenue sharing to Edward Jones.

What does this sentence mean?

Essentially, if you do not pay Edward Jones additional compensation via revenue sharing, they aren't going to allow their financial advisors to offer that mutual fund to you. Simply put, you as the client are not going to be offered lower cost mutual funds because those funds cannot pay Edward Jones any additional compensation.

Take a look at the next highlighted sentence. This one is my favorite!

> We want you to understand that Edward Jones' receipt of revenue sharing payments creates a potential conflict of interest in the form of an additional financial incentive

This is flat out saying, "We understand these additional fees are a conflict of interest" but we do not care! We want the additional revue. Either pay us or we will not offer your funds to our clients! How serious is this conflict of interest?

> For the year that ended on December 31st, 2020, Edward Jones received revenue sharing payments of approximately $247.9 million from mutual fund and 529 product partners and $4.7 million from annuity product partners.

Well, I would argue that $250 million dollars per year is a pretty serious conflict of interest.

When choosing who you want to partner with for your financial future it is important that you understand the distinct difference between a captive financial advisor (who must follow rules like what we have just covered) and an independent advisor who works only for the client, not the parent company.

Chapter 6

Wealth Advisor vs Retirement Planner

So, you have narrowed your search! You have decided you want to use a captive advisor or an independent advisor. Now what?

The next thing you will need to decide is what stage of life you are in, and what is important to you. From here, you have another two options:

- Wealth advisor or retirement planner

What do I mean by that?

Like the medical field, advisors specialize in different things. Would you go to your family doctor if you needed heart surgery? Probably not! Just like you would not go to an eye doctor if your knees hurt. Think back to Chapter 2, when we discussed your goals— strategies—tools.

When you define your goals, the strategies start to define

themselves. If your only goal at this stage of your life is the grow your wealth—than a wealth advisor might be the best option for you!

Wealth advisors spend their lives focused on the tools that are most efficient in growing your wealth. These tools include stocks, bonds, mutual funds, ETFs, real estate investment trusts (REITs) —the list goes on and on.

What you will notice when you break down each investment opportunity that a wealth advisor uses is that they all carry different degrees of risk. Stocks are typically riskier than bonds. REITs carry risk, but it is a different type of risk than that carried by mutual funds. The job of a wealth advisor is to balance out the risk versus reward that a client is seeking using the various tools in his or her toolbox. The wealth advisor will also focus on diversifying your risk by using different asset classes or sectors of the stock market.

How does a wealth advisor know how much risk you are willing to take?

Most are going to provide you with a risk questionnaire. This questionnaire is centers around five to seven questions designed to assess your willingness to take risk. Essentially, the goal of this questionnaire is to place you into one of five categories:

- Conservative
- Moderately Conservative
- Moderate
- Moderately Aggressive
- Aggressive

Stop right here for a second. Think about what just happened. You answered five to seven questions and all the sudden your "ideal" portfolio was born!

Wait, what?

You heard me correctly. Those five to seven cookie-cutter questions just determined your investment strategy. If you are a conservative investor, you will have about 70 percent of your assets in protected or stable investment tools. The other 30 percent of your assets will be in tools designed for growth, like mutual funds or equities.

Typical investment models based on risk assessment look something like this:

- Conservative = 70% Stable/30% Growth
- Moderately Conservative = 60% Stable/40% Growth
- Moderate = 50% Stable/50% Growth
- Moderately Aggressive = 40% Stable/60% Growth
- Aggressive = 30% Stable/70% Growth

Again, if your only goal at this stage of your life is to grow your wealth, this type of financial planning works great!

But what if you are at a different stage in your life? What if growing your wealth is no longer your primary goal? What if you want to retire and start taking income from your accounts? If you have paid into Social Security, when should you file for your benefits? When you placed your funds into your IRA or 401k, you did not pay any taxes. When should you start withdrawing from those accounts and paying Uncle Sam? If you are 65 and eligible for Medicare, do you need a supplement insurance plan? What supplement plan makes the most sense for you and your family?

If you are working with a wealth advisor, he or she will do their best to provide you answers. However, if we go back to our medical analogy, this would be like asking your family doctor to perform open heart surgery. During twelve years of medical school, your doctor learned how to perform the surgery, but has never performed the surgery. Your doctor can try, but is that the best option for you and your family?

Probably not!

If you are transitioning to a different stage of your life—a stage that is going to require more strategies than simply growing your wealth—maybe you need to change financial advisors as well.

This is where a retirement planner might be the best option for you. Retirement planners specialize in helping individuals plan for—you guessed it—RETIREMENT!

When you transition into the world of the permanently unemployed, your goals change dramatically! It is no longer about how fast you can run the race—how large you can build your portfolio. You have made it to the finish line! At this point it is about slowing down, protecting your wealth, and developing an income strategy that you can rely on!

Retirement is challenging—and so is the process to plan for it correctly. Over the next few chapters we are going to address what I call the five key areas of retirement so that you don't run into any issues like John and Diana did when planning their retirement.

The five key areas of retirement planning are:

- Income Planning
- Investment Planning
- Tax Planning
- Estate Planning
- Health Care Planning

When thinking about retirement, you should have a written plan for all five of these areas.

CHAPTER 7

Income Planning

Income planning is the foundation to your overall retirement plan. After all, the best income plan in the world is not very helpful if it runs out of steam before you do.

For much of history, retirement income was not an issue. As we discussed previously, individuals worked basically until death. Once Americans started planning for a true retirement – meaning they stopped working when they still had a number of years left – planning for income in retirement became a larger necessity.

At first, employers shouldered this responsibility through something called a pension. A pension is an employer-provided income stream that is paid to you until death.

In the 1970s, nearly 45 percent of private sector workers had a pension in America. That meant, for many savers, thinking long-term on income wasn't an issue. In fact, it wasn't something individuals had to plan for at all because their former employer did it for them!

That all changed in 1978 when Congress passed The Revenue Act of 1978, which added section 401(k) to the Internal Revenue Code.

Under these new plans, it was up to the employee- not the employer – to think long-term about income. A company would contribute money to an employee's qualified account, but it was up to the employee to grow that money and manage it so they'd have enough income to last a lifetime.

We transitioned from a system of defined benefits (where a company provided you a set income amount) to a system of defined contributions (where a company provided you a set amount to save each year). This was a fundamental shift in how Americans had to plan for retirement.

By 2017, only 13 percent of private-sector employees had a pension. While public-sector employees still often have pensions, many government pensions at the municipal, state, and federal levels are underfunded. Meaning, they cold potentially run out of money and not have the ability to pay former employees their pension payments

If you are lucky enough to have a pension, it is important for you to know if that pension plan has enough money to meet their obligations.

Because pension plans are a thing of the past, the responsibility has shifted to you to develop your own income plan in retirement.

Where should begin when building your own retirement income strategy?

I hate to say the "B" word, but having a BUDGET is vital in retirement. While working, if you overspend during the month or have higher than expected bills, you can simply pick up an additional shift—work some overtime— or pull from the emergency fund that you have built up. Whatever solution you choose, it is much easier when you can replenish your reserves from outside sources. While retired, the only source you have is YOUR retirement savings. Every time you dip into those savings to pay for unexpected or unplanned for expenses you are putting the long-term success of your plan in jeopardy!

Our planning process always starts with your day-to-day income needs. Think of these as your fixed costs to keep a roof over your head, food in your belly, and so on. How much does it cost for you to live the life you are used to?

If you have no clue, that is okay! You are not alone. Many of the individuals I meet with on a day-to-day basis have no clue how much their lifestyle costs them. Although you have never had to think about it in the past, now that you are retired or planning for retirement you MUST know your monthly income needed so let's start there!

Below is a worksheet that I use with my clients to determine their lifestyle needs in retirement.

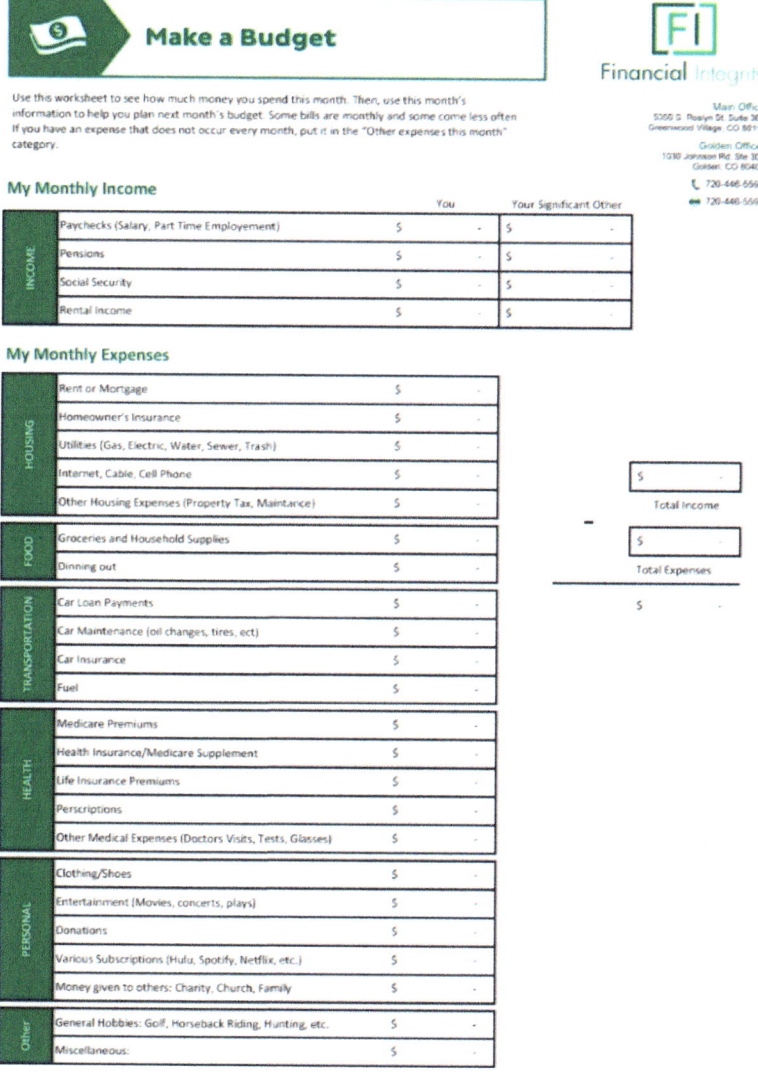

If you took the time to fill out our budget worksheet, congratulations! Whether this was the first time that you have sat down and really thought about your "budget" or simply took some time to update your budget, you have now taken the first step to planning your financial freedom in retirement! Now what?

It is time to start putting a plan together to get the monthly income you need! The typical retiree has three sources of income in retirement: Social Security, pensions, and retirement savings. Many call this the "Three-Legged Stool" of retirement.

You are probably thinking to yourself, wait! I only have two legs to my stool—I do not have a pension!

As discussed previously, this is the first major difference in retirement planning between you and previous generations. Starting in the mid'70s, employers shifted away from the traditional pension because it created a HUGE business liability.

As individuals started living longer in retirement, companies had to pay out pension benefits for longer periods of time. If you do have a pension, consider yourself lucky! As of 2017, only 16 percent of Fortune 500 companies still offered a pension to their employees. (Source: Willis Towers Watson report accessed June 1st, 2021.)

Without a pension, the burden of providing you the income needed in retirement falls onto the remaining two legs of your retirement stool: Social Security and savings.

In America, 97 percent of employed individuals pay into Social Security and are eligible to receive benefits in retirement. Among individuals older than 65, 50 percent of married couples and 70 percent of unmarried persons receive HALF or more of their monthly income from Social Security. For nearly 1 in 3 Americans, Social Security is their only source of income. (Source: https://www.ssa.gov/news/press/factsheets/basicfact-alt.pdf accessed 6/3/2021)

Although Social Security plays a pivotal role in the overall success of your retirement plan, what I have discovered is that very few individuals think through the decision of how to access this income. The information about when to file for Social Security is typically limited to the chart below. This chart illustrates that the longer you wait, the more you get!

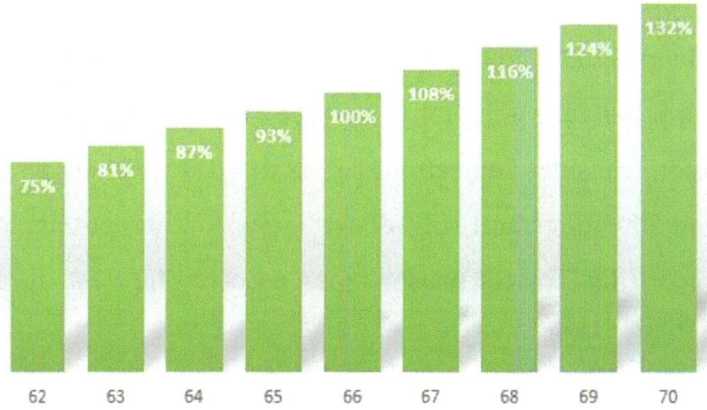

When discussing Social Security planning, everything is based on your Full Retirement Age or FRA. Your FRA is unique to you based on the year you were born.

The below chart will help you determine your FRA.

Year of Birth	Full Retirement Age
1938	65 years and 2 months
1939	65 years and 4 months
1940	65 years and 6 months
1941	65 years and 8 months
1942	65 years and 10 months
1955	66 years and 2 months
1956	66 years and 4 months
1957	66 years and 6 months
1958	66 years and 8 months
1959	66 years and 10 months

Has it always been this difficult to determine your FRA?

No, when Congress changed the FRA from 65 to 66 back in 1983, they wanted to implement those changes gradually. This same concept happened again when Congress changed some of the filing options back in 2015. If you were born prior to 1954, you can still use strategies like "file and suspend." If you were born after 1954, these strategies are no longer available to you.

Why do I bring this up?

Because individuals preparing for retirement often tell me that they want to file for Social Security at 62, the earliest date possible. When I ask why, they will often say because they are concerned Social Security is going bankrupt and they want as much from the system as possible before they shut off benefits.

Yes, Social Security is currently running a deficit (paying out more than it is taking in), which is a HUGE problem that Congress needs to address. But notice two things from the previous examples.

1) Changes to Social Security are implemented over time—not all at once.
2) Changes to Social Security calculations or strategies have never affected individuals 10 years or less from retirement.

Congress understands how important Social Security is for aging Americans. It understands individuals need time to plan for retirement. By looking at the changes Congress has made to the program, it is safe to say that your benefits are not going to be affected if you are 50 years or older currently. DO NOT make your decision to file for Social Security based on fear or emotions—let math and financial science determine when it is right for YOU to file your benefits. There are hundreds of calculators available that can help you determine your retirement benefits, break-even points, and so on, but those only look at your situation from a surface level. You really should consult a retirement planner to determine what is best for YOU based on longevity, retirement assets, and taxes.

Once you have determined what is best for you and your situation regarding filing for Social Security, it is time for step 3—solving your monthly "income gap."

How do you calculate your monthly income gap?

Monthly Income Need (–) Social Security (–) Pension = Monthly Income Gap

This is why we focused on creating your monthly budget earlier! Without knowing your monthly income needed, it is impossible to complete this equation. If your current financial advisor has never asked about your monthly budget or allowed you to give a vague answer, that is a pretty good sign you are working with a wealth advisor—not a retirement planner!

Now that you are making progress in building your income plan, and you understand your monthly income gap, how do we solve it? No matter who provides you with financial guidance in retirement, there are only three options available to you.

1) Develop a portfolio focused on rate of return
2) Develop a portfolio focused on dividend income
3) Invest in a private pension annuity or lifetime income annuity

Each of these strategies has pros and cons, which we will discuss in detail. What I want to stress is that you make this decision based on what is important to YOU and your family. It is not based on how your financial advisor gets compensated. Unfortunately, when it comes to this step of the planning process financial advisors tend to persuade their clients one way or another based on how the advisors are licensed. ALWAYS make sure you are working with a fiduciary.

Option #1: Develop a Portfolio Focused on Rate of Return

This is the most popular strategy for retirees today. Essentially, you build a portfolio designed for growth, take your monthly income as a withdrawal, and hope that everything works out okay in the long run.

Does it work?

Historically speaking, yes. There have been numerous research studies performed on this method, which is typically referred to as "the 4 percent rule." These research studies conclude that if you build a balanced portfolio of 60 percent stocks and 40 percent bonds and withdraw only 4 percent per year, your likelihood of not running out of money is relatively high!

How high might you ask?

Back in the mid '90s when William Bengen first published his famous 4 percent rule, the probability of success was nearly 100 percent in providing retirees a consistent income stream for 30 years of retirement. Today, many experts believe that withdrawing 4 percent is no longer as reliable as when Mr. Bengen first published his research study. Because of low interest rates, increases in inflation, and longevity (sometimes beyond 30 years), the new "safe" withdraw rate is 2.8 percent.

This means that if you build your retirement plan using option #1 you will need to allocate approximately 40 percent more of your retirement savings than previous generations if you want the same probability of success.

Example:

- $1,000,000 (x) 4% = $40,000
- $1,428,571 (x) 2.8% = $40,000

Pros of using the Rate of Return Method:

1) Provides a clear direction for amount that can be withdrawn from a portfolio
2) Monthly income is designed to increase with inflation
3) Maintains a high degree of flexibility and liquidity to make changes in the future

Cons of using the Rate of Return Method

1) Historical data from 1926 to 1976 was used to determine the probability of success

2) Probability is correlated to market performance, which is unpredictable

3) Decreases in portfolio value could lead to decreases in monthly income

How often do my clients choose this method to solve their income gap in retirement?

To be honest, it is rare that my clients choose this route to fill their monthly income gap. Remember, we are discussing strategies to maintain your lifestyle, keep a roof over your head, and put food in your belly. Most of our clients want their monthly income to be consistent and predictable, which simply is not possible when using an unpredictable investment like the stock market. So, when do clients choose this route? Typically, it is when they need very little income month-to-month. Their Social Security and/or pension covers most if not all their daily living expenses. They want supplemental income but do not actually need the extra income.

Option #2: Develop a Dividend Portfolio

What is a dividend?

- A dividend is a sum of money paid regularly (typically quarterly) by a company to its shareholders out of its profits (or reserves). Source: Oxford Dictionary

When companies become more established like Microsoft, McDonalds, and Walmart, investors understand that they are no longer going to grow by more than 30 percent every year as these companies did in the early days. Instead, these companies attract investors by making direct payments to shareholders in the form of a dividend from the companies' annual profits. These distributions are typically paid on a quarterly basis and are published months in advance of the payment.

Unlike the Rate of Return method, using a dividend portfolio does create predictability. Each company declares a dividend rate and the date that the dividend will be paid!

What would be the negatives to going this route?

Although a company has performed well in the past—and had the ability to reward shareholders with a dividend—it is not guaranteed the company will continue to do well in the future. Think about all the great companies that no longer exist today like Blockbuster or

Toys 'R' us. Also, during economic downturns like those in in '08 and during the COVID-19 pandemic, companies aren't as profitable. They might have to decrease or even eliminate their dividend completely.

To reduce the impact on your portfolio of a company going out of business or decreasing its dividend payments, it is crucial that you are well diversified and investing in strong companies when using this strategy.

Some examples of companies currently paying dividends:

Company	Dividend Rate (as of June 2021)
IBM	4.89%
Chevron	4.92%
Verizon	4.32%
Coca-Cola	3.19%
Procter & Gamble	2.89%
Citigroup	2.80%

Typically, a well-diversified dividend portfolio will provide you an annual dividend yield of approximately 3 percent to 3.5 percent.

If we use the previous example of a $40,000 per year income gap, you will need to invest between $1,142,857 and $1,333,333 into the dividend strategy to fill your income gap.

- $1,333,333 (x) 3% = $40,000
- $1,142,857 (x) 3.5% = $40,000

Although you can concentrate your portfolio on higher-dividend-paying companies so that you can create more monthly income, remember that there is a higher degree of risk with that investment. Many of my clients use the dividend approach to solving their monthly income gap if they understand a few things.

1) Because dividend rates are low (2 percent to 4), a large amount of capital must be invested to generate the income needed.

2) Although we can buy and sell different companies within the portfolio, this money is not a liquid savings account you can pull from. The money must stay invested to generate the dividend payment.

3) During bad economic conditions like COVID-19 or 2008, clients will need to take their monthly income from other sources because most companies are going to suspend dividend payments for a period.

One of the best benefits of using a dividend portfolio in retirement, if you are okay with the above, is that your original investment is never depleted. For clients looking to pass assets down to the next generation, this is a great way to build your income plan! Also, if you are using after-tax assets from your portfolio, dividends receive special tax treatment that we will talk about in the tax chapter of this book.

Option #3: Purchase a Private Pension or Lifetime Annuity

Uh-oh! I said the "B" word (budget) earlier and now I am saying the "A" word (annuity). This is supposed to be a family friendly book about retirement!

Trust me, there are some *TERRIBLE* annuities out there, just like there are some terrible mutual funds or terrible REITs (Real Estate Investment Trusts). However, there are also some good options for annuities if you understand how they work. Instead of thinking of an investment as good or bad, try to think of it as a tool that has a specific purpose with both pros and cons.

Why would you consider using an annuity?

Generally speaking, there are two purposes for an annuity.

1) Safe growth: We will discuss this type of annuity in more detail in the next section of this book.

2) Lifetime income: Guaranteed, predictable income no matter how long you live.

Let us examine how annuities work when your purpose is lifetime income. If you are fortunate enough to have a pension through your employer, congratulations! As I said earlier, pensions are extremely uncommon today. Instead, employers have elected to match your retirement contributions up to a certain percentage of your overall income. Essentially, they are trying to help you build your retirement savings faster so that you could use option #1 or option #2 that we just discussed.

But what if you do not like option #1 or option #2? You like the idea of having a guaranteed monthly income stream like a pension. Do you still have that option?

Ding, ding, ding! That is where a lifetime income annuity comes into play. Essentially, you take a portion of your retirement savings and exchange it for monthly payments that you can never outlive! You no longer need to worry about how long you are going to live, what the stock market is going to do, or if you will run out of money. All of those risks are transferred to the insurance company!

Sounds great, right?

Well, there are some disadvantages to using annuities to fund your lifestyle in retirement.

1) Once you make the decision that you want to use a lifetime annuity, that decision is very hard to reverse. Annuities have surrender charges or penalties for you to exit the contract.

2) Because these are insurance products, the younger you are, the less attractive they might be for your situation. Consult a financial advisor to receive a price quote based on your situation.

The clients that benefit the most from using option #3 to fill their income gap are the clients that just want to enjoy retirement stress free. They do not want to think about the stock market—they do not want to worry about how long they will live. They simply want to receive a paycheck every month to cover life's expenses. Annuities are the most restrictive way you can build a retirement plan (because of the surrender charges) but they are also the most predictable route you can go to generate the monthly income you need.

Quick recap of your three options to fill your monthly income gap:

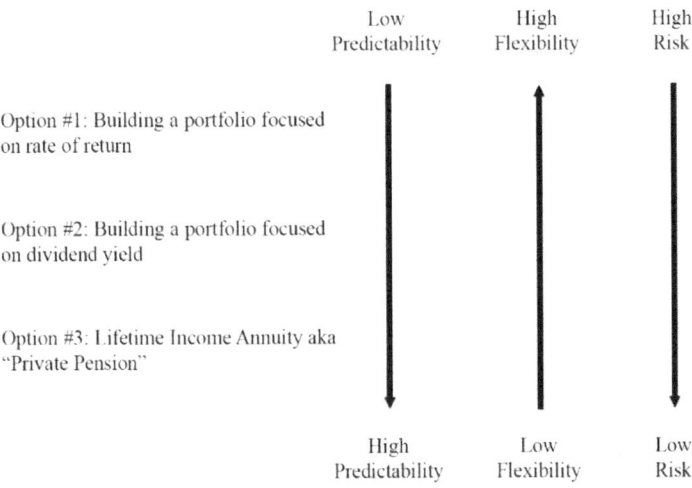

Everyone and their situation is unique. Everyone has different goals and concerns when entering retirement. Because of that, no two solutions will be the same. To me, it is more important that you are educated about the pros and cons of your investment decisions and together we build a plan that best accomplishes your goals!

CHAPTER 8

Investment Planning

Turn on Fox News or CNN. Pick up the Wall Street Journal or the New York Times. Open your hometown newspaper. What will you likely see? Discussions about the stock market.

I don't know if you are readying this book while the market is up or if the market is down. If the commentators believe we are in a bull market or a bear market. What I do know however, is that everyone has their opinion about the stock market, and everyone likes to share their opinion. Most of which are completely different than the next person you listen to.

I have been personally trading assets in the stock market since I was 13 years old. I will be the first to admit, the stock market is tricky! It can change dramatically year by year (sometimes day by day), making future projections a challenge.

For me, it is better to look at the stock market long-term. No one has a crystal ball that can predict the stock market day by day or even year by year for that matter. But if you look at the stock market over a longer period of time it becomes more predictable.

Look back at the 1990s. The '90s were booming days in the market. You might remember something called "Dart Funds." These were funds where a stockbroker literally threw a dart at a sheet of stocks and invested in whichever ones the dart hit. You know what? Dart funds were making good money! Everything was making good money. The market was going up, up, up!

We all know what happened after the feel-good years of the '90s – the "dot-com" bubble burst. We started the new century in 2000 with three straight years of market losses. From March 2000 to October 2002, the NASDAQ lost 78 percent of its value. The S&P 500 fell nearly 40 percent. Many people's retirement accounts were severely depleted. A running joke at the time was that 401(k)s had been reduced to 201(k)s.

After years of increasing interest rates through the '80s and '90s, the Federal Reserve decided to lower interest rates in 2002. This provided stability to the market, and we began to recover from 2002 to 2008. Those years were years that many people spent just trying to claw back what had been taken during the dot-com collapse. Suddenly, the real estate bubble burst and sent the market crashing again. This time, it fell fast! The S&P 500 lost 37 percent of its value in just a few weeks.

Again, the government went to work. Congress passed stimulus packages, bank bailouts, and other forms of new spending. The Federal Reserve lowered interest rates once again – this time to historic lows.

From 2009 to 2020, the stock market experienced a historical bull run! Interest rates have remained incredibly low, quantitative easing has continued. Even though we had recovered economically from the 2008 collapse, every government official has made sure to not let the economy stubble on their watch – no matter the cost…

How long can the government support the stock market? I think the better question is, does the government have the ability to help us recover from next recession?

The swift and extensive action taken during the COVID crisis erased a 26 percent loss in just 3 months. But at what cost? Nearly $5 trillion in national debt. Lowering interest rates to essentially zero. Printing 30 percent of the entire world's money supply in 12 months. Do they have anything arrows left in the quiver?

This is where I have major concerns for investors today. You might be thinking it is ok to continue taking risk in the stock market because "it always comes back over time." Which is correct, but how long are you willing to put your lifestyle on hold while you wait for it to come back?

This is the very reason that I teach my clients to focus on income planning first. Develop a predictable and sustainable income plan that is independent of your investment plan. Make sure, not matter when the next recession hits or how long it lasts that you do not have to put your lifestyle on hold.

This is another area where retirement planners differ from wealth advisors. Instead of investing all your assets based on your risk questionnaire, retirement planners will segment different sections of your assets and invest them toward your investment goals. If it only takes 15 percent or 20 percent of your portfolio to obtain your income goals, why are 100 percent of your assets invested the same way? That seems extremely inefficient to me!

Typically, when an investment is good at one thing (such as creating income) it is terrible at something else (such as long-term growth).

Because of this, I segment each area of your retirement plan to focus on the best investment tools designed to meet that purpose. To help my clients understand this process of segmenting assets, I use the term "fiscal house."

Just as each section of your house is designed for a different purpose—that is, the kitchen is where you make food, and the bedroom is where you sleep—each section of our fiscal house has a specific purpose!

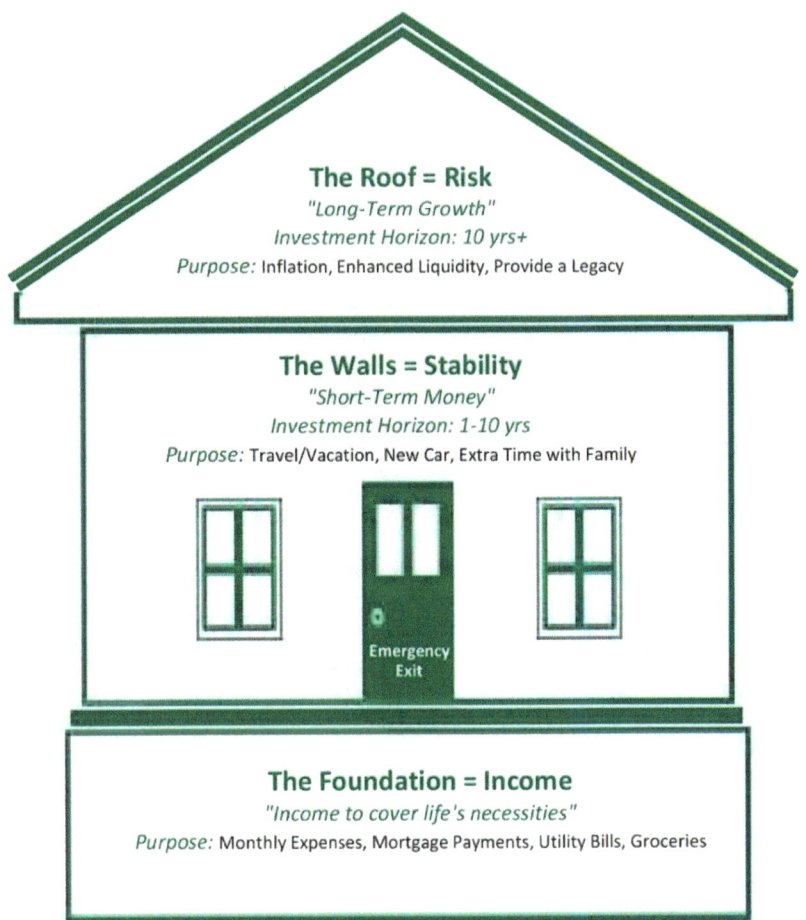

The Foundation

The foundation of our fiscal house is focused on generating monthly income to fill your income gap. This is what we discussed in the previous chapter. Once you determine your monthly income gap, and the strategy you want to use to solve that gap, we need to invest the correct percentage of funds into that strategy to accomplish your goals.

The Emergency Exit

Everyone needs to have cash in the bank to cover the little things that will come up in life. You never know when you will need a new hot water heater or new tires on the car. Typically, I suggest individuals keep between three and six months' worth of expenses in cash reserves. Because of inflation, you do not want to keep to more than that in cash, as it is a depreciating asset.

The Walls

You did not work for more than thirty years to sit at home and look at the TV while you age (at least I hope not). What do you want to do with your newfound time and freedom? What places do you want to see? What things do you want to accomplish? Do you want to make some renovations to the house or possibly buy your dream car to drive through the mountains?

When building my investment plans, I have my clients complete what I call the "Bucket List" exercise. It is a simple worksheet that forces you to sit down and plan out all the items in your life that you want to experience, but could not enjoy while you are working.

Below is an example of our "Bucket List" worksheet for you to use.

Main Office
5350 S. Roslyn St, Suite 360
Greenwood Village, CO 80111

Golden Office:
1030 Johnson Rd, Ste 330
Golden, CO 80401

📞 720-446-5595
📠 720-446-5597

Retirement Bucket List

What do you wish to accomplish?	How much will it cost?
1)	$
2)	$
3)	$
4)	$
5)	$
6)	$
7)	$
8)	$
9)	$
10)	$

Investment advisory services offered through AE Wealth Management, LLC an SEC Registered Investment Advisor

Take some time right now to complete this exercise. I have my clients think about the next ten years of their life for this exercise.

We call this the "go-go years." Once you have completed this worksheet, add up how much all your bucket list items are going to cost you over the next ten years.

The approximate cost of your bucket list is how much you need to have invested in your walls. You see, to us the purpose of the walls isn't about rate of return (also known as growth), but rather the enjoyment you receive by fulfilling your dreams. What I have learned while helping people retire is that money loses its importance over time, but memories are forever!

The goal of the walls of our fiscal house are to keep your money safe, offset inflation with a growth goal of 3 percent to 5 percent, and most importantly keep your money liquid so it is ready to spend when you are ready to spend it.

Without completing this exercise—without knowing how much money you want to spend over the next ten years on your bucket list items—without earmarking those funds to pay for the trips or dream car, I can say with pretty good confidence that those dreams will go unfulfilled. The saddest part of my job is working with individuals who were too scared to spend their money early in retirement because they did not want to run out, but no longer have the health to enjoy the things they put off while they were working.

So, what investment tools can you use for the walls of your "fiscal house?"

Traditionally, individuals have used CDs, cash, or bonds for stability and safe growth. Let's take some time to examine these options.

Cash - I am confident that the most used term in the financial world is, "cash is king." But is it?

Cash does serve a purpose. It allows you to cover life's emergencies. It is 100 percent liquid and safe from market loss. Many will also argue that it also allows you to take advantage of investment opportunities when they present themselves.

Let me ask you a few questions. How much do you have in cash right now? Is it more than 3 to 6 months' worth of living expenses?

If so, you have more than what is needed to cover emergencies so you must be waiting for the opportunity to invest those funds. If that is the case, how long have you been waiting? Think about how much the stock market is up over that time meanwhile you've been earning 0.008% at the bank.

Trust me, I understand you want to keep this money safe and do not want it in the stock market, but cash is not the right answer either. With inflation increasing, every day you leave money in cash at an interest rate lower than inflation, you are losing buying power.

CDs –A CD is an investment in which you form a contract between you and the bank. Essentially, you lend your money to the bank for a set period of time. The bank then lends your funds to other individuals.

In return, the bank will provide you interest for allowing them to use your funds. Back in the '80s and '90s when interest rates were high, you could ladder CDs at 6 percent and simply live off the interest that the bank was paying you.

Today, a 3-year CD generates less than inflation. Instead of calling these Certificates of Deposits, we now refer to them as Certificates of Depreciation.

Bonds – Bonds are by far the most common investment vehicle used by investors today for providing stability from market volatility. Over the last 30 years, bonds have provided investors a predictable return between 3 percent and 5 percent.

Will that stable and predictable return provided by bonds over the last 30 years continue for the next 30 years?

To answer that question, you first need to understand what a bond is. Bonds are a contract between you as the investor and an underlying institution such as a company or government entity. These institutions issue a bond because they are trying to raise money for certain projects.

If you purchase a government bond, your funds are typically used to fund new roads and bridges or to keep the government funded for general operating expenses.

If you purchase bonds issued by a company, your funds are typically used to develop a new product or expand into new markets and create additional profits for the company.

As the investor, you are the banker. When determining which bonds to purchase you are analyzing the interest rate the institution is willing to pay you for lending them your funds along with the ability of that institution to pay your funds back to you lending period is over and the bond has matured.

The more stable of company or institution that you choose to lend your money to the less interest rate they will pay you as an investor. If a company or institution is unstable and has risk of not being able to repay your bond at maturity, they will need to pay a higher interest rate to attract investors.

Below outlines the different ratings placed on bonds and the risk involved with each.

Fitch	S&P	Moody's		Rating grade description (Moody's)
AAA	AAA	Aaa		Minimal credit risk
AA+	AA+	Aa1		
AA	AA	Aa2	Investment grade	Very low credit risk
AA−	AA−	Aa3		
A+	A+	A1		
A	A	A2		Low credit risk
A−	A−	A3		
BBB+	BBB+	Baa1		
BBB	BBB	Baa2		Moderate credit risk
BBB−	BBB−	Baa3		
BB+	BB+	Ba1		
BB	BB	Ba2		Substantial credit risk
BB−	BB−	Ba3		
B+	B+	B1		
B	B	B2	Speculative grade	High credit risk
B−	B−	B3		
CCC+	CCC+	Caa1		
CCC	CCC	Caa2		Very high credit risk
CCC−	CCC−	Caa3		
CC	CC	Ca		In or near default,
C	C			with possibility of recovery
DDD	SD	C		
DD	D			In default, with little chance of recovery
D				

Bonds have an interesting relationship to interest rates. Most would think that if interest rates go up it would have little impact on bond prices, but that is not the case. Bonds have an inverse relationship to interest rates.

Think about it this way. When a company issues a bond, they are trying to attract investors to purchase the bonds. As an investor, you are always weighing the risk vs reward to decide where to invest. If you can get 6% keeping your money at the bank in a CD, why take the risk of buying a bond that is only paying 4%? As interest rates rise for other forms of "safe" investments like CDs or savings accounts, institutions or companies have to raise the interest rate they reward investors in order to attack those investors. If a company has to pay a higher interest rate back to an investor, that leaves them less money to invest toward the purpose that the bond was issued in the first place for.

Because of this relationship, as interest rates rise – bond prices fall in value.

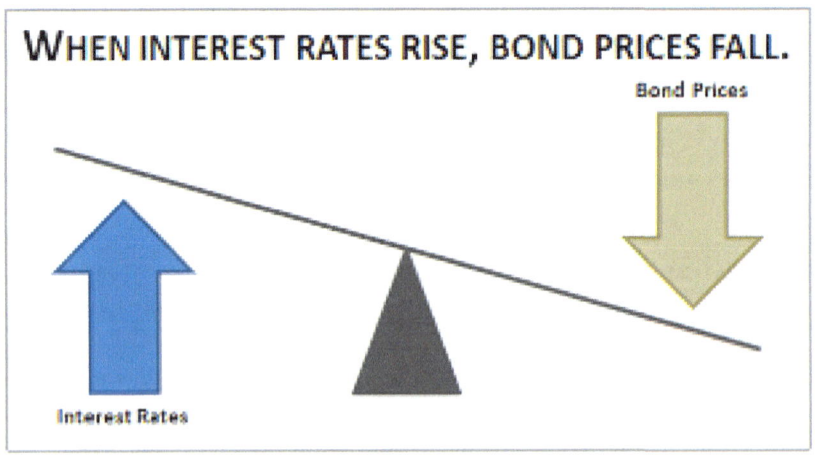

Ask yourself, what were interest rates in the '80s and '90s?

A mortgage for a home was around 12 percent. Banks were offering CDs at 6 or 8 percent. Because of the inverse relationship of interest rates to bond prices, that means bond prices were extremely low back in the '80s and '90s.

Remember from our previous chapter how the Federal Reserve choose to lower interest rates in 2002 so that we could recover from the dot-com recession?

Well, that caused bond prices to increase. In 2008 and 2020 when the Federal Reserve choose to lower interest rates yet again – that pushed bond prices even higher.

During the COVID crises, interest rates fell to nearly zero meaning that bond prices were at all-time highs.

At this point, bond prices can only increase in value if interest rates go negative - which we will have a completely different problem on our hands if that happens!

Because of low interest rates, experts predict that you will average around 1.8% yield on investment grade bond portfolio over the next 10 years. If you are willing to except default risk, and purchase high yield bonds, experts only predict your portfolio to earn around 3.5% over the next 10 years.

Think about that for a second. Right now, you probably have 30 percent or maybe even 40 percent of your portfolio in an asset class that is only expected to earn 1.8 percent.

On top of that, you are paying your financial advisor an advisory fee to invest your funds, probably around 1 percent. That means your net yield, after paying advisory fees, is only 0.8 percent! If you then factor in inflation, which is higher than 0.8 percent, you are losing buying power every year (and paying someone to lose it for you).

Although bonds have worked for past generations, they will not work well for future generations. Can you really call a bond a "safe" investment if you are almost guaranteed to lose buying power when you factor in inflation? The rules of investing have changed, and for you to have success, your investments must change as well.

What alternatives do you have outside of Banks or Bonds?

Until around 1995, the answer was essentially nothing. Investors were stuck between a rock and a hard place. Accept the risk or accept zero return.

What happened in 1995?

Well, interest rates were so high that companies were struggling to offer competitive bonds that would attract investors. Couple that with the need for greed (the '90s were a great time for investing in the stock market) and it was almost impossible to raise capital!

Enter, insurance companies. They understood the need for greed and higher returns but also understood that not everyone enjoys putting their money at risk. What if they could couple the two? What if they could offer protection similar to a bank savings account or CD but also offer the ability to grow similar to the stock market?

From this concept developed by insurance companies, the Fixed Indexed Annuity was born.

Protect the client's money from loses in the stock market, but if the stock market goes up 25 or 35 percent, which was common in the '90s, allow the client to earn 15 or 20 percent. Insurance companies could not offer them all of the potential growth of the stock market, but investors were okay with that because they did not assume any risk!

What seemed like an amazing opportunity for investors was slow to become mainstream. Financial advisors saw Fixed Indexed Annuities as competition to the bonds that they were offering to their clients. Millions and millions of dollars were spent by brokerage firms to spread negative information about this new investment opportunity. Unfortunately, it was not until after investors lost over 40 percent of their assets within a ten-year period (2000 – 2002 and

2008) that Fixed Indexed Annuities gained in popularity.

In the year 2020, nearly $220 billion dollars were invested into Fixed Indexed Annuities based on LIMRA's estimates of the total annuity sales market.

Why have Fixed Indexed Annuities gained so much traction with investors over the past 20 years?

Personally, I think there has been a dramatic shift in education. Individuals like yourself have concerns about their financial wellbeing and are becoming more involved in the investment process. Instead of just handing the keys over to their investment advisor, they are asking questions and seeking alternatives.

Savers today face something no other generation has faced: the conflux of a volatile stock market and persistently low interest rates.

In Modern Portfolio Theory (which is just a fancy way of describing how financial advisors balance risk and protection in an investor's portfolio), the traditional solution for retirees is adjusting your asset allocation between stocks and bonds. The typical portfolio design is 60 percent stocks and 40 percent bonds. If your current financial advisor has never discussed the risk associated with bonds today and presented alternatives like an annuity, that is a pretty good sign that you are not working with a fiduciary (as discussed in previous chapters).

Are all annuities good? Do they all work the same way?

Absolutely not! For every good annuity available to investors there are two not so good options. If you are interested in discussing annuities as a potential investment for your retirement portfolio, please consult an independent advisor that is licensed with multiple insurance companies so that you can get the best option for your situation.

The Roof

The last and final stage of building your investment plan is the roof. Until this point, we have solved your day-to-day income needs using the foundation. We have earmarked money to fund your bucket list goals inside of the walls. You have three to six months' worth of expenses in the bank to cover the "what-ifs" that life is going to throw your way in your emergency exit. Whatever is left, whether that is 10 percent of your portfolio or 90 percent, does not matter. This is the money that you can afford to put at risk.

The one and only purpose of the roof is long-term growth. Because of how we have developed our clients' fiscal house, they understand that these funds are not needed for more than 10 years. This allows us to invest these funds with a higher degree of risk because we now have time on our side to weather the ups and downs of the stock market. Again, this is a huge difference between retirement planning and wealth planning. Because wealth planners traditionally leave all of your eggs in one basket designed around your risk tolerance, you diminish your own returns! By focusing each section of your fiscal house to perform a specific task, it not only has the potential to increase your overall portfolio returns, but it increases your peace of mind.

When the country first went into lockdown due to COVID-19 and the stock market plummeted more than 30 percent in a matter of weeks, I started calling all my clients to make sure they were okay with everything and see if they had questions. I will never forget a conversation that I had with Linda. As soon as I told her why I was calling she said, "Cody, unless my foundation and walls are going to collapse, I'm fine! Don't waste your time calling me, I know I am okay!"

I often reflect on that conversation for a couple of reasons. When I first met Linda, she was a recent widow. While alive, her husband handled all the finances and investments. When he passed, Linda panicked. She pulled all their investments out of the stock market and put them in cash. If she did not understand how something worked, she wanted nothing to do with it! At least if it were in cash, she knew she could not lose it. When COVID hit in March of 2020 it was the quickest 20 percent market correction in American history. When I called Linda, who just 3 years ago hated the stock market, she said, "I'm not worried about it!" That is the power of proper investment planning. That is the power of education!

CHAPTER 9

Tax Planning

We have now come to my favorite part of planning a long-game retirement: Taxes.

It's not because I love taxes. In fact, I don't enjoy them much at all. I hate owing them, and I hate paying them.

Rather, it's because this is the chapter where I get to try and fundamentally change the way you think about retirement. Most of you at least think about market volatility when planning your retirement. Most of you have at least considered how to make your assets last for the rest of your lifetime.

You know what many of you probably have never considered before? The impact of taxes on your retirement.

Your Hidden Debt:

You have probably heard of Dave Ramsey. He is an author, radio host, TV star, and popular purveyor of financial advice. If you have ever listened to his show, you know his most famous piece of advice:

Get out of debt!

Ramsey encourages Americans to pay off their credit card debt, car loans, medical bills – even their mortgages.

In general, it is good advice. Americans carry way too much debt and paying some of that off is good for you long term. What I am alarmed by is that Dave Ramsey completely overlooks one of the biggest debts nearly every American carries today. Tax Debt.

What do I mean by tax debt? You do not owe the IRS anything. You pay your taxes every year. How dare you tell me to pay off my tax debt!

In this chapter we are going to discuss taxes and their impact on your retirement income.

Most individuals have very limited knowledge about how taxes are calculated. You have never had to worry about it before! You have allowed your employer to do the calculations for you, deduct from your paycheck what it is owed, and then come April you cross your fingers for a refund!

When you enter retirement, you no longer have an employer. It is now completely on your shoulders to estimate your taxes, have them withheld from your income streams, or pay quarterly estimates. Beyond just having to calculate and withhold the correct amount, taxes are MUCH more complicated once you enter retirement because you are no longer receiving your income from a single source. You now may have pension income, dividends, capital gains, Social Security, required minimum distributions, or Roth distributions. Each of these different sources are treated differently by the Internal Revenue Service (IRS). If you understand how the tax code works and the relationship between these different sources of income, you can save yourself thousands of dollars in taxes!

Very few individuals reading this book are certified public accountants (CPAs) nor do they want to be. My intent is not to turn you into a CPA during this chapter, but rather cover at a general level these different sources of income so that you can build a more efficient tax plan in retirement.

Why are taxes and tax planning so important for you to understand while planning your retirement?

From my time on earth, I have learned that actions in Washington often have long-term consequences. Although the psychological and health ramifications of COVID will be with us for some time, the biggest long-term impact will be how the government responded.

Within weeks, businesses and schools closed. Cities shut down. The global economy came to a complete standstill. Unemployment spiked and the stock markets dropped 26 percent. The outlook was dire for our national economy.

So, congress got to doing what Congress does best: spending money.

In response to COVID's economic impact, the government passed several stimulus packages aimed at supporting unemployed workers and struggling businesses.

The price tag of the initial stimulus package was around $2.2 trillion. This spending increased unemployment benefits, provided Paycheck Protection Program (PPP) loans, and expanded Medicaid access.

It also added TRILLIONS of dollars of new debt to the national deficit.

Government spending is a common way countries battle the economic impact of disruptive events like COVID. Both George W. Bush and Barack Obama ushered in large stimulus packages to address the 2008 recession.

COVID-related spending has eclipsed almost anything our country has ever experienced in the past in both size and speed. In fact, the stimulus spending incurred during 2020 generated the most deficit spending the U.S. has incurred in modern history.

What impact will this spending have on your retirement?

Back in March of 2020, a reporter asked U.S. Treasury Secretary Steven Mnuchin if he was concerned about the deficit. After all, the government had just added two trillion dollars to our nation's already massive IOUs.

Mnuchin acknowledge the historic deficit spending, and then added: "In different times, we'll fix the deficit. This is not the time to worry about it."

Did you catch that?

Secretary Mnuchin did not say, "We don't have to worry about the deficit," or "We have a plan to resolve the growing deficit." He simply stated that now is not the time to worry about the deficit. We will address the deficit when the time is right.

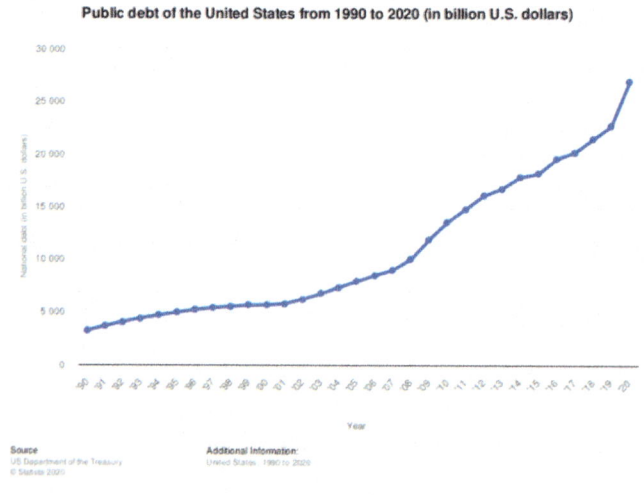

Public debt of the United States from 1990 to 2020 (in billion U.S. dollars)

So, how will America address our ballooning deficit?

America can reduce our deficit in several ways, so let's look at the options and their likelihood of addressing our current national debt.

1) Reduce Government Spending – The government can reduce its deficit by reducing the amount of money it spends each year. While this sounds appealing in theory, in practice it is difficult for even the most fiscally committed President to achieve. That is because the majority of the U.S. spending is not dependent on new laws or spending bills Congress and the President can control. Mandatory government spending – which includes Social Security, Medicare, Medicaid, and the interest on current government debt currently consumes 60 percent of all spending. Today's voters are asking for even more government spending, not less. To me, it is highly unlikely that we see a dramatic reduction in government spending which leaves this as an ineffective way to lower our national debt.

2) Quantitative Easing – The 2008 recession was the first time most Americans heard the term "quantitative easing." Essentially, quantitative easing is when the government issues bonds to borrow money then buys back those bonds with newly issued money (aka printed money). As we witnessed after the 2008 recession, this approach helped, but it's not perfect. The economy strengthened but not at the

same pace as the presses were printing the money to strengthen the economy. Because of this, our deficit grew. Also, the reactive measures of quantitative easing to pull us out of the 2008 recession were never lifted. Even though the economy strengthened, the government continued printing. This imbalance causes inflation, which is a completely different risk to your retirement.

3) Taxes from Economic Growth – New tax revenue generates money the government can use to pay down the deficit. As our economy expands, new jobs are created, new transactions occur, and new services are purchased. All has the potential of creating new tax revenue. Unfortunately, it is unclear how soon sustained, robust economic growth will return. Which leads us to...

4) Taxes from Individuals – Here is an approach we have seen time and time again. Our government wants to spend more money. How does it get more money to spend? It raises taxes on Americans. Sometimes this is through adjusting tax brackets, and sometimes this is through other changes to the U.S. tax code. Either way, the result is more tax revenue for the IRS and potentially less money for you to enjoy your retirement!

To further discuss how you could potentially be affected by changes in the U.S. tax code, I think it is important that you understand how the IRS views your assets and how they are taxed.

I always start off by discussing what I call, "The Three Tax Buckets."

Every asset that you have saved to this point in time in your life can fall into one of these three buckets. Each bucket has its own tax rules, so it is important that you understand each classification of money.

The First Tax Bucket: Tax Deferred

As you can probably imply from the name of this bucket, you have never paid tax on any of the assets currently inside this bucket. When you invested the funds, Uncle Sam allowed you to defer your taxes until a later date. The earliest that you can withdraw from these funds, without using special IRS rules, is the age of 59 ½. If you withdraw funds from your tax deferred bucket prior to the age of 59 ½ you will pay not just ordinary income taxes on the withdrawal, but you will also be subject to a 10 percent tax penalty for withdrawing funds early. If you retire pre-59 1/2 there are some special tax laws that can allow you to take funds early, but special conditions must be met. If you are in this position, talk with your

CPA or financial advisor for more information.

So, you can't take funds pre-59 ½, but you also can not just leave the money sitting in this bucket forever. Uncle Sam was nice enough to allow you to defer those taxes while you were working, to allow them to grow faster for you, but at some point, Uncle Sam wants you to pay the taxes you owe! When must you start taking funds from your tax deferred bucket? It used to be age 70 ½; however, that law has since been changed to age 72. Once you reach this age, you must start withdrawing funds annually by December 31st. These withdraws are referred to as RMDs or required minimum distributions. You can take out more than your RMD, but you cannot take out less. If you take out less than what the government requires, you pay a 50 percent penalty! Yes, you read that right—50 percent!

Obviously with that stiff of a penalty, you want to make sure that you calculate your RMD correctly, so how do you do that?

Easy! First you need to calculate how much you have in all of your tax deferred accounts. The IRS uses the value on December 31st of the prior year. This calculation includes all your 401k's, IRAs, savings, 403bs—and anything else. Once you have calculated the total amount that you have in all your tax-deferred accounts, you simply divide it by how long you are going to live. That sounds silly, right? You don't know how long you are going to live! That is correct, you do not know how long you are going to live, but the government thinks it does. The government has published what is referred to as the Uniform Life Expectancy table.

	New Uniform Lifetime Table				
Age	Uniform Table RMD Factor	RMD as a % of Account Balance	Age	Uniform Table RMD Factor	RMD as a % of Account Balance
70	29.1	3.44%	96	8.3	12.05%
71	28.2	3.55%	97	7.8	12.83%
72	27.3	3.67%	98	7.3	13.70%
73	26.4	3.79%	99	6.8	14.71%
74	25.5	3.93%	100	6.4	15.63%
75	24.6	4.07%	101	5.9	16.95%
76	23.7	4.22%	102	5.6	17.86%
77	22.8	4.39%	103	5.2	19.24%
78	21.9	4.57%	104	4.9	20.41%
79	21	4.77%	105	4.6	21.74%
80	20.2	4.96%	106	4.3	23.26%
81	19.3	5.19%	107	4.1	24.40%
82	18.4	5.44%	108	3.9	25.65%
83	17.6	5.69%	109	3.7	27.03%
84	16.8	5.96%	110	3.5	28.58%
85	16	6.25%	111	3.4	29.42%
86	15.2	6.58%	112	3.2	31.25%
87	14.4	6.95%	113	3.1	32.26%
88	13.6	7.36%	114	3	33.34%
89	12.9	7.76%	115	2.9	34.49%
90	12.1	8.27%	116	2.8	35.72%
91	11.4	8.78%	117	2.7	37.04%
92	10.8	9.26%	118	2.5	40.00%
93	10.1	9.91%	119	2.3	43.48%
94	9.5	10.53%	120+	2	50.00%
95	8.9	11.24%			

Source: Internal Revenue Service, Updated Life Expectancy and Distribution Period Tables Used for Purposes of Determining Minimum Required Distributions. November 8, 2019

Your current age is represented on the far-left hand side in the first column. The number of years that the government things that you have remaining is in the middle column. The approximate percentage amount that you will need to withdraw is reflected in the far-right hand column.

If you are 72 years old, the government predicts that you will live 27.3 more years. Pretty specific if you ask me! One you take another trip around the sun; you are now 73 years old. Well, the government only predicts that you will live another 26.4 years. Essentially, every year that you gain in age, they subtract one year from your life expectancy.

Example of how to calculate your RMD

- Tax Deferred accounts as of Dec 31st = $500,000
- You are currently 72 years old, so you divide the $500,000 by 27.3
    - So, your RMD that year is = $18,350

The next year, you would again calculate all your Tax Deferred accounts but now you would divide the value by 26.9 because you would be 73 at that time!

The rules that are important to understand for this bucket are:

1) All distributions taken are classified as ordinary income and will be taxed as ordinary income.
2) You MUST start distributions at 72 whether you need the income or not
3) There is a 10% tax penalty for taking distributions pre-59 ½

The Second Tax Bucket: After-Tax

Unlike the first bucket, in which you defer the taxes owed until you withdraw funds, this bucket of money has already been taxed. Typically, this happens when you spend less than you make. Eventually your savings will grow to a point where it will start to earn interest (as little as that is today) or you will invest those funds into other investment vehicles like the stock market or real estate.

Since most of my clients invest these funds into the stock market, let's use that as our example to better understand taxes on assets. Real estate has a few different rules.

Remember, these funds have already been taxed before based on your income level when the money was earned. Typically, you have already paid between 12 percent and 30 percent in taxes on these funds. But that doesn't mean you never have to pay taxes on these funds again. The big issue with this bucket of assets is that when you invest the funds, you now pay additional taxes on the growth of those investments. That is right—they will be taxed again! The government classifies these taxes as capital gains taxes.

There are two types of capital gains, and they are taxed differently. Short-term capital gains: These are gains that are realized within a 12-month period. The government does not provide any special tax treatment for short-term capital gains and treats them as ordinary income. Based on your income level when the gain is realized, this could be another 12 percent to 30 percent! It is important if you are managing your accounts yourself that you understand this rule. Any time you buy and sell something within 12 months, it is going to show up on your tax return as ordinary income.

Long-term capital gains: If an investment is held for twelve months and one day, the IRS provides the investor special tax treatment using the long-term capital gains tax brackets. Below is an example of those backets for both a single individual and a married couple filing jointly.

Married Filing Jointly	
Captial Gains Thresholds	
$0 - $80,800	0%
$80,801 - $501,600	15%
$501,601 +	20%

Single Filing	
Captial Gains Thresholds	
$0 - $40,400	0%
$40,401 - $445,850	15%
$445,851 +	20%

What you have probably noticed from the above chart, is that there is a tax bracket in which you can realize a long-term capital gain and pay ZERO in income tax. For the tax year 2021, that threshold is $80,800 for a married couple or $40,400 for a single tax filer. I would also like to note that the $80,800 and $40,400 is in addition to your standard deduction. This means that if you are a married couple filing jointly and your income is below $105,000 approximately or $55,000 for a single person you can realize long-term capital gains up to that threshold 100% tax free!

Think about your conversations with your current financial advisor. When you have asked about tax reduction strategies, what answer do you typically get? I'm guessing, it sounds something like this, "Well, taxes aren't my area of expertise. You will need to discuss that with your CPA."

Let me ask you something: when was the last time your CPA helped you buy or sell stocks or other investments?

You see, what typically ends up happening—especially in retirement when taxes are so important—is that one professional you work with (your financial advisor) passes the buck to another professional you work with (your CPA) who then passes the buck back to your financial advisor. It is like an endless game of hot potato! Unfortunately, this leaves you stuck in the middle, and you never receive the tax help and guidance that you need to take advantage of some of these strategies! While you were working, it probably was not as important that the financial advisor you employed understood tax laws. But, when you retire and now have control over how you pay Uncle Sam, it 100 percent matters that your financial advisor not only understands tax law but is proactive in helping you manage your investments in a tax-efficient manner.

The Third Tax Bucket: Tax Free

As the old saying goes, nothing in life is free. That is especially true when it comes to your money. One way or another, you are going to pay taxes.

This bucket is like the after-tax bucket that we just discussed. When you earn the funds or place outside funds into your tax-free bucket, you are responsible for paying the tax bill prior to depositing the funds. The big difference, though, between this bucket and the after-tax bucket—these funds are never taxed again! It doesn't matter if you take the funds out during your lifetime for monthly income or to fund a big vacation, or you happen to leave these assets to the next generation. It is all 100 percent tax free!

The most well-known investment vehicle for tax-free money is known as a Roth IRA. Like the traditional IRA, you only pay taxes once. Taxes are paid when the funds go into the bucket for a Roth versus taxes being paid when you take funds out of a traditional IRA. Both seem to be the same, right? You still must pay taxes.

Being a farm kid, I like to use this analogy to help clients understand the difference between the two. With a traditional IRA, the government allows you to go to your local Co-Op or seed store and purchase the seeds you wish to plant without having to pay tax on the seeds. The government understands that it's hard to be a farmer.

You plant the seeds and hope that they grow, but there is no guarantee! Seems reasonable, thanks big government for understanding!

So, you get the seeds tax free, but as those seeds start to grow and turn into a beautiful field of wheat, corn, or sorghum, the government wants to share in that success! They gave you the seeds tax free, but now they are going to collect the tax on your harvest.

A Roth IRA is the exact opposite. Instead of you getting the seeds tax free from your local seed supply store, you go ahead and pay the taxes owed for the seeds that you receive. Now, when those seeds start to grow and produce that amazing crop you have been farming, you do not have to allow the government any of your success!

Think about that analogy. When do you have more seeds to be taxed? Is it before you plant them in the ground or is it after you have spent time tending and watering the fields to create an amazing crop? Obviously, it is before you grow the crop!

This is why I stress the importance of Roth IRAs to my clients. Even if you are currently in retirement and you have never placed funds into your tax-free bucket, it is not to late! You can convert from your traditional IRA to your Roth IRA, pay the taxes today on those "seeds" and let the Roth IRA grow tax-free from this point forward! Think about how well the stock market has performed over the past ten years. Your "field" or tax-deferred portfolio has grown well, I assume. All the growth your accounts have experienced have simply grown the amount you will eventually owe to the IRS. Why not reverse course now? Pay a little tax on some "seeds" and get them into a Roth conversion so that you can stop growing your tax bill.

Now that you understand, at least at a high level, the three tax buckets and how the IRS taxes these assets, it is time to share one more item that is valuable to developing your income plan in retirement. That bit of information is how taxes are calculated on your Social Security benefits.

As we discussed in the previous chapters, almost everyone in America is eligible for Social Security benefits yet almost no one understands how they are taxed. Again, my goal is not to turn you into a CPA, but I do want you to understand the correlation between tax planning and income planning in retirement.

Social Security is taxed using a calculation referred to as provisional income. What is provisional Income and how is it calculated?

There are four items that go into this calculation

1) 50 percent of your Social Security benefit
2) Ordinary income
3) Dividends and capital gains
4) Non-taxable interest

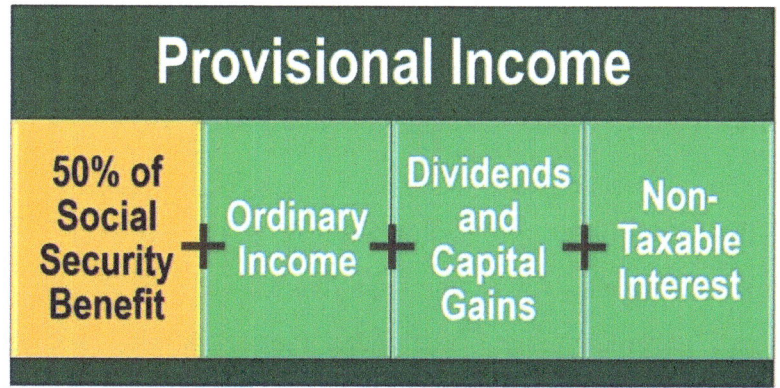

Did you know that your Social Security benefit itself could cause you to pay additional taxes on your Social Security benefit? Unfortunately, that is exactly how the tax code is written. This is another reason why we typically have individuals delay Social Security when we are doing advanced tax planning strategies.

Ordinary income is any IRA distributions, including RMDs; any pension payments you receive; and any employment income, whether it is part time or full time.

I discussed dividends and capital gains in the after-tax section of this book. Most of the individuals I meet have portfolios that are generating dividends, but they are reinvesting those dividends. I consider these phantom income taxes. Not only are they potentially paying capital gains taxes on the dividend payments, but they could also potentially be creating additional taxes due on Social Security benefits. I always inform clients, if you are not using your dividends to supplement your monthly income as we discussed in Chapter 7, get those dividends off of your tax return! Again, this is another area of planning that is 100 percent the responsibility of your financial advisor. Your CPA does not help you invest your assets.

Finally, let's look at non-taxable interest. Some higher net worth individuals are attracted to municipal bonds. These are investment vehicles that create federal tax-free income but can also avoid state income taxes if the bonds are purchased in the state in which you claim your primary residence. Even though the interest is tax free, the interest is used in calculating the taxes owed on your Social Security. Remember that if you have municipal bonds inside your portfolio, as it decreases the after-tax yield of those bonds and might make them less attractive to own.

OK, you have your provisional income number—now what?

There are two thresholds the IRS uses based on your provisional income number to determine how much of your Social Security benefit you will need to claim on your tax return.

Social Security Provisional Income Tax Thresholds

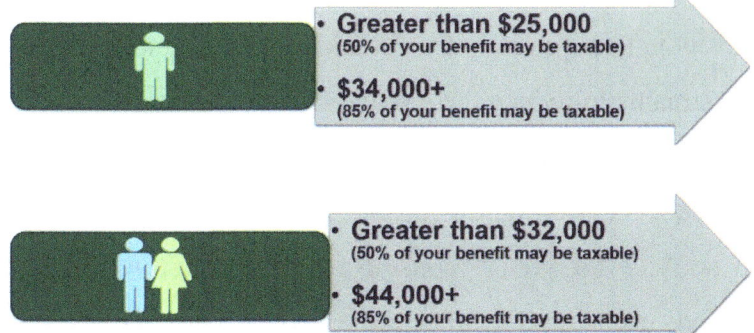

Source: Social Security Administration (SSA), www.SSA.gov

What this graphic illustrates is that if you are single individual with a provisional income number above $25,000, 50 percent of your Social Security benefit above that threshold becomes taxable as ordinary income. If you cross $34,000, 85 percent of your Social Security benefit now becomes taxable as ordinary income. For a married couple, the 50 percent threshold is $32,000 and the 85 percent threshold is $44,000.

Without proper income planning, it is inevitable that your Social Security benefits are going to be taxed. If you work with a qualified retirement advisor that understands the relationship of these different income streams and how they affect your provisional income calculation, it is possible to avoid paying taxes on your Social Security benefits!

There is a saying that the only two things in life that are certain are death and taxes. Although you cannot avoid paying taxes, you can be efficient in how you invest your funds and how you develop your income streams to reduce the amount that you are required to pay. Unless you are the type of person who wants to pay Uncle Sam more than you are required (and I haven't met anyone like that yet), it would be wise for you to consult a retirement professional that understands taxes to see if there are ways that you can reduce your long-term tax obligations.

Retirement Readiness Quiz

We have made it—well, you have made it! I hope you were able to gain some valuable knowledge from this book that puts you on the path to financial freedom in retirement. To gauge how ready you are, here is a quick checklist you can use:

1) Have you created a monthly budget to sustain your lifestyle in retirement?

2) Have you determined the best strategy for you to claim Social Security benefits?

3) Do you understand and feel comfortable with your income strategy to fill your monthly income gap?

4) Have you created a bucket list of items you want to accomplish in retirement?

5) Have you earmarked money inside of your portfolio to fulfill those bucket list items?

6) Are you taking advantage of the historically low tax rates to position yourself better long-term?

What are our clients saying about Financial Integrity?

FI has been a wonderful resource for financial planning and investment opportunities. My advisor Cody Meeks has been an outstanding, knowledgeable, value driven advisor with a personal touch. I would recommend FI for your future financial planning and investment needs.

~ John D.

I was ready to retire, but not sure if I could financially afford to do so. Luckily, I had gone to a Financial Integrity seminar and heard Cody speak. He talked in terms I could understand, and I made an appointment. We looked at my numbers and I was able to retire at 62!

Two years later I am enjoying life and my retirement! And, I didn't have to change my lifestyle!

All thanks to Cody Meeks and Financial Integrity!

~Pat B.

I was very limited on my financial knowledge especially was I was nearing retirement. Cody was very patient, and knowledgeable as he led my wife and through financial education based on our current portfolio.

His guidance was very realistic, based on principles, had products to help meet financial goals and set up a sound retirement plan.

His clear explanation helped us see our financial reality and give us a handle on the remaining working years and how to manage finances once I retired.

~ Dan & Lyndi O.

My wife Laurel and I have been clients of Cody Meeks for nearly 3 years. Cody is personable and truly knowledgeable about current tax laws and up to date on a variety of financial issues. We feel like he is always looking out for our best interests.

Cody's explanation of his financial philosophy is clear and easy to understand. He is well prepared for our meetings and responds quickly when we try to get in touch with him. We would not hesitate to recommend him or Financial Integrity to anyone looking for a Financial Advisor.

~ Rod & Laural S.

I first met Cody Meeks of Financial Integrity in 2018 when I was half-heartedly looking for a new financial advisor. I had been using an advisor that I had been turned over to when my original advisor retired.

She was adequate but never seemed to make clear certain investments, or move me out of previous old investments, which I later learned were not in my best interest (through no mal-intent on her part). As luck would have it, I happened to attend one of Cody's dinner talks and learned more about investing in that one evening than I had in all the years with both my previous investors. Cody's knowledge of the industry, enthusiasm and willing to work with my needs and market anxieties have continued to impress and reassure me, especially in these rocky times.

I appreciate his accessibility, his patience with my repeated questions, his transparency and his frequent offers to review my portfolio. Cody has become more than my trusted financial advisor, he has become like trusted family.

~ Linda R.

After listening to several informative sessions from different financial advisors, we feel so lucky to have found Financial Integrity. Cody listens to our needs, our feelings about risk, and our hopes. He answers our questions with honesty and an expertise that we trust. It almost feels like we are with family.

~ Frank & Stacey H.

When we started looking for a financial adviser, we didn't have a clue where to even start!

When we met Cody Meeks at a retirement seminar, we knew we were going down the right path! He has helped us in getting all of our assets under one roof and to help us realize we are fully prepared for the next phase of our life - retirement!

~ Jack & Linda H.

Made in the USA
Columbia, SC
08 November 2022